GOOD SHEPHERD CONVENT
ST. LOUIS
PROVINCIAL LIBRARY

ON THE THEOL____ ____EATH

D0166549

236.1
21.5 cm

236.1
R33
058

ONVENT

RARY.

ABOUT THIS BOOK

The author treats from the theological point of view of
the nature of the Christian's death and of the special
mode of death called martyrdom. He is concerned with
opening up new perspectives in older problems, striving
to formulate new and more fruitful concepts for the
penetration of one of the most important dimensions of
Christian belief and experience. Writing with the great
care necessary in theological discussion yet abstaining
from technical terminology and jargon, he conveys a
sense of the intellectual urgency and the exploratory
nature of the inquiry.

This book forms part of a series of short treatises entitled
Quaestiones Disputatae in which some of the more urgent
open questions of the Christian faith are discussed by
eminent Catholic writers.

QUAESTIONES DISPUTATAE

IWWCI USENTHR O

KARL RAHNER

ON THE THEOLOGY
OF DEATH

889

1090

150.

HERDER AND HERDER

GOOD SHEPHERD CONVENT
ST. LOUIS
NOVITIATE LIBRARY

HERDER AND HERDER NEW YORK,
232 Madison Avenue, New York, N. Y. 10016

Original edition "Zur Theologie des Todes", Herder, Freiburg.

1st English Edition 1961
Translated by C. H. Henkey
2nd Impression 1961
3rd Impression 1962
4th Impression 1963
5th Impression 1964
2nd English Edition 1965
revised by W. J. O'Hara
2nd Impression 1967

Nihil Obstat: Hubertus Richards, S.T.L., L.S.S.
Censor deputatus
Imprimatur: E. Morrogh Bernard
Vic. Gen.
Westmonasterii, die 4a aprilis, 1961

The Nihil Obstat and Imprimatur are a declaration that a book or pamphlet is considered
to be free from doctrinal or moral error. It is not implied that those who have granted the
Nihil Obstat and Imprimatur agree with the contents, opinions or statements expressed.

Library of Congress Catalog Card Number: 61-11443
First published in West Germany © 1961 Herder KG
Printed in West Germany by Herder

CONTENTS

INTRODUCTION

In seeking to come to some understanding of the theology of death, it is necessary to make some prefatory observations which will forestall misunderstanding of the aims and limits of our proposed investigation. Theology and faith, without question, belong together. Nevertheless, they are not the same. Faith is the assent, the "yea", of the whole man to the message of God which we receive as the word of God from the mouth of the Church. Theology, on the other hand, is the methodical attempt to secure an explicit understanding of what has been heard and accepted as the word of God. Because the word of God can only be accepted by faith when it is to some degree understood, faith can never proceed wholly without theology. Nor can theology proceed without faith, since it presupposes hearing the word of God. Nevertheless, faith and theology are not identical. The understanding of God's message heard and believed, which reflection and methodical scientific research can secure, varies a great deal in extent and degree. The correctness of this understanding will, accordingly, be guaranteed by the Church to a varying degree. At the very inception, consequently, of a topic belonging both to faith and to theology, we are confronted by a problem of method. When, for example, a Catholic theologian attempts to treat of death, should he confine his attempt to discussing, as clearly as possible, whatever is contained, as a matter of fact, formally

7

and explicitly, in the teaching of the Church and in the Bible? Should he enunciate only what he has directly "heard"? Or should he also discuss the results of his own theological work, by which, without the formal sanction of the Bible and the teaching authority of the Church, he tries to attain a better understanding of what he has "heard"? I have in mind that kind of theological work which only begins when the doctrine of the Church has been clearly determined, and compares the single propositions of this doctrine with each other, confronts them with other types of knowledge and goes on to elaborate more fully the concepts they involve, in order to secure a more precise understanding of what has been directly heard in faith. The two methods of approach, that of faith and that of theology, are basically inseparable and can only to a certain degree be kept apart. Nevertheless, they are not the same, and we must decide which we are to employ.

We are perfectly aware that the first undertaking, that is, as objective as possible a presentation of what is immediately and explicitly contained in the actual sources of faith concerning death, would be a considerable task in itself. We shall, nevertheless, attempt the second task, as far as the limits of space will allow, and seek to formulate a "theology of death" in the proper sense of the term. We make such a choice chiefly because in this way precisely with regard to this topic it is possible to arrive at an understanding of the common belief of the Church concerning death, which a simple exposition of the express doctrine of the Church on the matter would perhaps not provide to the same extent.

Once this choice has been made, some further brief remarks on the method proper to such an effort are in order. The point of departure for the reflections of the Catholic theologian is always the doctrine proposed by the ordinary and the extra-ordinary *magisterium* of the Church to the faithful and to the theologian alike, as the content of revelation in Scripture and Tradition. The doctrine proposed by the *magisterium*, once the theologian has determined what it is (and this deter-mination may at times, according to the matter involved, be a formidable task), becomes the unquestionable foundation for all further efforts by the theologian. Just as the theoretical physicist relies upon the data of experiment, so for the theo-logian, official Church doctrine is a fact which he takes as a starting-point of reflection, not an opinion which he discusses. What the attitude of the Catholic theologian must be if this foundation is contested, and how he might justify his position, constitutes another problem which we cannot of course discuss here. But this fundamental position of all Catholic theological research, which holds for Catholic biblical scholarship as well, must be borne in mind to avoid any misunderstanding of what will be said concerning the theology of death. In view of this state of affairs it may well happen that theoretical theology will contain much that is unclear, inchoate, and problematic on some particular topic, even if the foundation on which it rests, namely, the explicit data of the Church's teaching to the extent that they are immediately evident, is relatively simple and clear. The reason is that such theoretical theology, while developed on the basis of Church doctrine, inevitably involves, implicitly or explicitly, consciously or unconsciously, the use and assistance of metaphysical methods, concepts, *aperçus* and theories extrinsic to theology itself. This will be seen to be the case with our present topic. It should cause no

9

astonishment, therefore, if what can be said consists to a great extent in listing (far from completely) theological questions relating to our theme rather than in supplying answers.

A final observation may be permitted by way of introduction. Death is one of the most shattering events in human life. It is not without significance that the Bible describes the human situation as "to sit in darkness and the shadow of death" (Lk 1:79). Our experience of history has thrown this shadow only too darkly over us. Consequently some may regard as revolting the attempt to describe death in an apparently existentially unconcerned manner, circumstantially and with an elaborate apparatus of metaphysical concepts and theological formulae, and to speak of it as though it were the slightest of human things, a commonplace object in regard to which philosophical and theological logic-chopping can be indulged without restraint. It is impossible to avoid creating such an impression. Nevertheless, if we do not wish to suffer death, around us and in ourselves, merely passively and in dull resignation; if as men, as spiritual beings, we must, and prefer to, face death with alert hearts and open eyes; and if, as Christians, we should know (as St. Ignatius of Antioch says in *Ad Rom.* 6:1), that "it is beautiful for me to die in Christ Jesus", then a theology of death, which does not shrink from sober conceptual elaboration, is both important and desirable, even though it seems to transform the experience and shock of real death into a phantom web of concepts and *theologoumena*.

With no further delay, then, let us address ourselves to the problem. On the one hand, we must begin by asking: what are the sure, clear statements of Christian faith concerning death? We shall not claim, of course, that such a list of statements or propositions comprises everything that in fact belongs to the content of Christian faith about death. In fact, much more may belong to it. But in the present stage of our faith and its explicit proclamation, at any rate, this is not so unambiguously clear. On the other hand, what we first expound belongs to the immediate substance of the Church's doctrine and is warranted by her teaching authority. What we have earlier called "theoretical" theology will then have to be added. Our method will be briefly to state, point by point, the clearly determined propositions of the Church's doctrine on death, attempting at each point to advance a little way further into the theological problems and speculations which are suggested by each statement or can be developed from it.

The advantage of this procedure is that the affirmations of the doctrine of faith will receive, in some measure at least, detailed and explicit consideration. A disadvantage, of which we are quite aware, is that this method does not permit a systematic presentation of the theory of death. It will not result in a clearly rounded, well-balanced, comprehensive theology of death. The explicit doctrine of the Church is not, however, determined by considerations of system. As the explicit understanding of divine revelation develops, the Church, in announcing and teaching it, emphasizes now one and now another portion of it, not according to the requirements of system, but according to the concrete necessities of the historical situation. As a result, we cannot expect an integral, systematic theology of death to emerge from the explicit statements of the faith concerning death, from which we take our point of departure. We can only make short separate excursions into a little-known territory, rather than undertake an exhaustive geographical survey of the whole region. Even to attempt the latter would be foolhardy. It is not feasible, by reason of the subject itself as well as of the limits of the present essay. Furthermore, an attempt to present a systematic account of the theology of death would unavoidably lead to the explicit doctrine of the Church being placed in the background and even more prominence given to private theological *theoremata* than these in any case will inevitably occupy.

Even so, however, a certain articulation follows from the subject-matter itself. Among the propositions of the Church's doctrine on death, some are, obviously, applicable to every human death; others qualify death in such a way that they cannot apply to every case. For example, Scripture speaks of the death of the sinner, a death which is the expression and consequence of human guilt. It also speaks, however, of a dying with Christ, when death no longer has the character of a penalty for sin. There are clearly, therefore, dogmatic statements about death as an event which is common to all and presupposed by the actual concrete condition of man, in regard, that is, to supernatural salvation. Other statements qualify death itself, differentiating it according to the relationship of the human being who dies to God. Such considerations determine our first, rough distribution of subject-matter. We must consider first those existentially neutral statements on death, which describe it as an event common to all men (Part I). We shall then consider death under its aspect as the decisive event for sinful man, in which man's sinful perdition finds its complete expression and retribution (Part II). Finally, we shall consider death as the supreme act of appropriation of salvation based on the death of Christ (Part III).

1. *The Universality of Death*

The universality of death is one of the affirmations of faith. Leaving aside the special question of the fate of those persons who will be alive at the consummation of the world through the second coming of Christ and who, according to St. Paul, will be transformed into the final stage of their bodily glorification without tasting death (1 Cor 15:51; 1 Thess 4:14 ff.), faith teaches that all men are subject to the law of death and that all men will, in fact, die. This proposition, though it seems to be knowable through a process of empirical induction, possesses, by reason of its source in divine revelation, an entirely different character from the apparently identical statement based on human experience. As divinely revealed, it embraces the entire conceivable human future and this is not really a matter of course; moreover it is given a special basis. Death and its necessity becomes more than an obscure, unsolved, purely biological problem, because the universality of death in divine revelation is not ultimately based on a biological necessity, but on something proper to man as a spiritual person in his relationship to God. All men are sinners, therefore all men die; and vice versa, precisely in the fact that all men die, there is manifested in the severest way in human experience the universal subjection of man to sin. The statement of faith concerning the inevitable universality of death and the reasons for it, is not at all affected by any possible outcome of the biological discussion (which is still far from settled) about the cause of death (death from physiological old age, that is); from the biological point of view this might be regarded as an "accident", or as the biologically inevitable end of a living being which as such is extended and oriented in time, and therefore has an end. Since we do not really know why all living things composed of many cells, and man in particular, do die, the reason offered by faith (that is, the moral catastrophe of mankind in its first parents) is really the only available explanation of the incontestable universality of death. And the theological ground includes the certitude that the necessity of death belongs to the necessary features of human existence and that it will never be possible to abolish death. Even if there is a natural explanation of the necessity and universality of death (whether in some chemical law or in some strictly biological necessity, in which latter case we should consider death not so much as a mere necessity as the fulfilment of a natural desire), it can still be said in justification of the belief in the universality of death that these natural causes of death would not have been able to operate in the condition of man in the Garden of Eden, because of an exceptional gift of God. Consequently, even the free operation of the natural causes of death can be traced to a cause in the moral and spiritual history of man. Though its execution occurs through natural processes, the death of man, in actual human history, has an ultimate, special cause. How the universality of death and the subjection of all men to death which it manifests, as well as the penetration of the whole of human life by death, actually affect the life of man, what positive and negative significance the finite character of man thus revealed has for the whole life of man, cannot be pursued further here.

2. Death as the Separation of Body and Soul

The dogma of the universality of death (prescinding for the moment from the reason assigned for this universality) describes the phenomenon of death from the outside, as it were, specifying merely the extent of the occurrence. A second proposition of faith, however, comes closer to the essence of death, even if it still considers human death from the point of view of his character as an organic being, and not from his specifically human, that is, personal essence. From this point of view, the traditional Catholic formula of preaching describes death as the separation of body and soul. This description is not as a matter of fact explicitly contained in Scripture itself. When, for example, the Old Testament (which, of course, knows of human survival after death), speaks of the return of the spirit in death to God (Eccl 12:7) and of the return of the body to the earth, it actually affirms explicitly nothing more than that God withdraws his life-giving power, and man descends into the grave. It does not formally state (nor, of course, does it deny) that the individual spiritual soul is separated from its body. The biblical expression, "to be dissolved" resounds in our ears, yet it should be recalled that this phrase does not actually translate the original with complete fidelity. The word used in the passages referred to (Phil 1:23; 2 Tim 4:6), in fact means "to set forth".

The description of death as the separation of body and soul is, however, used so much as a matter of course from the earliest Fathers down to the catechism of Cardinal Gasparri, that from the theological point of view we must consider it as the classical theological description of death. And it does, in fact, say something essential about death. It refers, first of all, to an indisputable truth, that the spiritual life-principle of man, the soul, assumes in death, to put the matter vaguely but cautiously, a new and different relation to what we usually call the body. The soul no longer holds the structure of the body together as a distinct reality, governed by its own immanent, vital laws and delimited from the rest of the universe. The body lives no more, and in this sense we can and must say that the soul separates from the body. And since it is a truth of faith (and no doubt of metaphysics as well) that the personal, spiritual soul does not perish when the structure of the body is dissolved, but maintains its personal, spiritual life, though in some wholly different manner of existence, this fact, too, finds clear concrete expression in the description of death as the separation of body and soul, for the term "separation" implies the continued existence of the separated elements. These two points of view, without doubt, supply an essential justification of this traditional description of death. Nevertheless, as theologians, we may point out that this is a description and nothing more, and by no means a definition of death in its very essence. The way is thus clearly open for very important further distinctions that may be drawn.

This description is certainly not an essential definition of a kind that would satisfy the demands of metaphysics or of theology. It is absolutely silent, for example, about the characteristic feature of death, that it is an event for man as a whole and as a spiritual person. Even if this description might be accepted as adequate for the biological decease of a man or of an animal, it fails completely to indicate the specifically

17

human element in the death of man. For, as we shall have to insist, it is *man* who dies. In death something happens to him as a whole, something which, consequently, is of essential importance to his soul as well: his free, personal self-affirmation and self-realization is achieved in death definitively. This should not be conceived as something occurring "with" death or "after" it, but as an intrinsic factor of death itself. But this decisively characteristic element of human death is not indicated at all by the expression, "separation of body and soul". Inevitably, too, the following problem must be raised: does the soul separate itself from the body, or is it separated from it? In other words, is this separation a result of the soul's own deeper dynamism towards its own fulfilment or is it something that supervenes upon the soul in opposition to its own innate tendency? The classical description of death leaves this too unanswered.

Moreover, it is an inadequate description, because it leaves the very concept of separation obscure, and leaves room for some very important distinctions. For since the soul is united to the body, it clearly must also have some relationship to that whole of which the body is a part, that is, to the totality which constitutes the unity of the material universe. This unity of the world, however, both metaphysically (on the basis, that is, of a scholastic metaphysics of *materia prima* and of a metaphysics of the very analogous concept of the "individual" material thing), as well as from the point of view of speculative cosmology, is not to be conceived as a merely conceptual sum of individual things, nor as the mere unity of an external interaction of individual things on one another. In the present context it is not possible to determine more precisely in predicamental terms in what the supra-empirical nature of this real, ontological unity consists. However, if the soul at any rate by its substantial union with the body as its essential form, also has a relationship to this radical unity of the universe, the question arises whether the separation of the body and soul in death also involves the definite cessation of the soul's relation to the world, so that the soul becomes a-cosmic, totally out of the world? Or does the termination of its relation to the body by which it maintains and forms the latter's structure and delimits it from the whole of the world, rather imply that it enters into some deeper, more comprehensive openness in which this pancosmic relation to the universe is more fully realized? In other words, does the soul in death strictly transcend this world or does it rather, by virtue of the fact that it is no longer bound to an individual bodily structure, enter into a much closer, more intimate relationship to that ground of the unity of the universe which is hard to conceive yet is very real, and in which all things in the world are interrelated and communicate anteriorly to any mutual influence upon each other?

This question is of course unusual in theology and in Christian philosophical anthropology. The separation of soul and body is usually taken almost as a matter of course to imply that the spiritual soul becomes acosmic. This conception prevails because instinctively or, to speak more precisely, under the persistent influence of a Neoplatonic mentality, we tend to assume that the appearance of the soul before God, which, as faith teaches, takes place at death, is a contrary concept to the soul's belonging to the world, as though lack of relation to matter and nearness to God must increase in direct ratio.

If, however, the metaphysical and religious problems created by such a tacit assumption are recognized and as a consequence a habit of thought in terms of this Neoplatonic ascent is overcome (it has lasted 2,000 years), the possibility of interpreting the description of death as the separation of soul and body in this second sense will become at least conceivable. One may even incline to accept the theory that in death the soul becomes not acosmic, but pancosmic, as theologically tenable.

The reasons are both ontological (in the sense of the philosophy of nature) and theological. We can here only briefly indicate them. The older scholastic doctrine concerning the relationship of body and soul did not conceive the informing of the body by the soul as an act distinct from the soul itself, an operation of a merely accidental kind, but as a substantial "act" of the soul, the very reality of the soul itself, to the extent that the soul's own substantial being is, so to speak, built into the material reality, as an act which is not really distinct from the soul. Such an act, consequently, could absolutely cease only if the soul itself ceased to exist. As a consequence, the older, strictly Thomistic metaphysics taught that even after death the human spiritual soul has a transcendental relationship to matter, that is, one posited by the very essence of the soul. This doctrine has only to be taken seriously, and "matter" understood in a more exact, ontological sense (rather than merely as indicating the concrete, measurable body), to recognize that the view here proposed is already contained in the strictly traditional Thomistic doctrine.

We might go on to consider a doctrine of "life-entelechies" and their relation to matter which has gained ground. This relation is conceived as reaching down to the ultimate, meta-empirical ground of material reality. The entelechies of sub-human living beings, therefore, do not appear merely as organizing principles, superimposed on an inorganic matter already formed chemically and mechanically; the at least partially supra-individual character of the sub-human ente-lechies must also be taken into account. This kind of idea makes it impossible to think of death in the sub-human realm, as the simple cessation of an entelechy (as the scholastic philo-sophy of nature used to hold), but death even in the sub-human realm appears as the surrender of the entelechical relation at a certain space-time point in the world, while the entelechical powers persist as constituents of the universe. If that is so, since the spiritual soul is a real life-entelechy (though that is not its only significance and despite the fact that the soul is essentially more individual than the entelechies of the sub-human realm), something analogous may be conjectured regarding the relation of the human spiritual soul to the world. The human spiritual soul will become not acosmic but, if the term may be used, "pancosmic". We might also simply raise here in passing the question whether, on this hypothesis, certain parapsychological phenomena might not be more easily ex-plained. Obviously this pancosmic relationship, which the soul always possesses, and to which it opens out in death, cannot be understood as meaning that at death the entire world be-comes the "body" of this particular soul precisely in the way in which its own body was its own. The pancosmic relation does not imply a substantial informing of the world in its space-time structure by the soul, in the way in which for scholastic metaphysics the soul informs the body. Nor, of course, is it

21

relation to the whole cosmos, might come to have a direct influence within the world.

The theological reasons for the interpretation of death as the separation of body and soul which is here proposed, must be indicated even more briefly. We may note, first of all, that a biblical, theological and, at the same time, metaphysically more profound study of the angels might suggest that the angels, too, prior to their actual individual spiritual decision and self-determination, and previous to any particular influence through efficient causality on individual things in the world, possess a permanent relation (though different in its orientation) to the world as a whole, which belongs essentially both to their nature and to the actual world itself. They do not exercise their activity and influence on the world merely occasionally (as though from some purely sporadic decision of their own); they belong to it permanently and continuously (not in spite of, but precisely because of their incorporeality). They are in fact principles ἀρχαί, κύριοι, κυριότητες, ἐξουσίαι, στοιχεῖα τοῦ κόσμου, κοσμοκράτορες, δυνάμεις: Col 1:16; 2:10; 2:15; 1 Pet 3:22; Eph 1:22; 3:10; 6:12; Jude 6; 1 Cor 8:5; 2 Pet 2:10; Gal 4:3, 9; Col 2:8, 20; Apoc 14:10) of the world, ultimate foundations of the natural order of things, precisely where it is a case of the natural and right order of events in this world, and they operate by reason of their essential relationship to the universe. The theological assurance of a natural, pancosmic relationship between the angels, as personal spiritual beings, and the world, makes it impossible to exclude, a priori, as an idea without parallel elsewhere, the possibility of some such relationship in the case of the spiritual, personal principle in man; or to preclude the possibility that in death it is not

23

abolished, but is rather, for the first time, perfected, becoming a fully open, pancosmic relationship, no longer meditated by the individual body.

This hypothesis would also render more readily intelligible the doctrine of purgatory. That doctrine implies a further maturing of man, even after death, though in accord with his final decision during life, through temporal punishment for sin (that is, the endurance of the repercussions of the world on the never perfectly right moral attitude of man).* This doctrine is perhaps clearer if it is assumed that the soul, freed from the body, is not removed entirely from the world, but that the soul, after surrendering its bodily structure and through that surrender, experiences in its morally free self-determination more clearly and acutely its own harmony or disharmony with the objectively right order of the world, and conversely, itself contributes to determining the latter. The following point must also be considered. According to the doctrine of the Church purgatory is the penal consequence, after death, of venial sins. In a Thomistic metaphysics, venial sins are only possible in a material being, that is, in a being which by reason of its materiality, which to a certain extent always resists personal self-determination, is capable of acts which do not involve a person's total disposal over his whole existence. Now if venial sin (of course only as regards its possibility) is the consequence of corporeality, is it not likely

---

* Cf. on this interpretation, which cannot be further developed here, a few indications in my essays: "Remarks on the Theology of Indulgences" in *Theological Investigations* II (London 1964), 175—201; "Guilt and its Remission: the Borderland between Theology and Psychotherapy" (*ibid.* 265—81); "Beichtprobleme" in *Schriften zur Theologie* III (Einsiedeln 1956), 227—45, especially 240 ff.

that undergoing the consequences of venial sin may involve as the very condition of its possibility, a human "corporeality" after death, though of an essentially different kind?

The resurrection of the body, at the end of the world, is a dogma of faith. Now if death, for reasons presently to be discussed, should not be conceived merely as something without purpose simply undergone by man, or as a destructive fate striking him from without, but is rather to be regarded as the accomplishment of the end towards which man positively strives, even though death in fact accomplishes this end in such a manner, interiorly speaking, that it can and does have a penal character; and if death as such an end positively aimed at were only a complete release from the body and a total departure from the world, then it would be difficult to see how the resurrection of the body could still be a positive component of man's perfection desired by the soul itself, and of the perfection of his personal, spiritual principle. Conversely, however, from the idea that such a new acquisition of bodily form in the resurrection is definitely not to be conceived as a surrender of the pure openness of the spirit to the whole cosmos which is attained in death, we might secure in principle a better basic understanding of the qualities of the glorified body as indicated in the sources of revelation (1 Cor 15). The transfigured corporeality of which revelation speaks seems to indicate that the body not only obtains a perfect plasticity in relation to the spirit of man as supernaturally perfected and divinized by grace, but also that corporeality does not necessarily coincide with the exclusion of localization in any other place. A corporeality which is the actual expression of spirit, though concrete, remains open for maintaining or entering into free and unhampered relations with everything. In this way the glorified body seems to become the perfect expression of the enduring relation of the glorified person to the cosmos as a whole. Other theological grounds for such a restricted or modified conception of death as the separation of body and soul must be omitted here for brevity's sake. We shall have occasion to return to them when treating of the redemptive influence of Christ's death on the world. We have dwelt in some detail on the theological difficulties involved in the traditional description of death as the separation of body and soul. We may now turn from this problem to list further some of the propositions on death which are directly perceptible in the tradition of the faith.

3. Death as Concluding Man's State of Pilgrimage

A third proposition of faith also views death under a formal, not a concrete individual aspect, though it regards man more as person than as nature. It affirms that with bodily death, man's state of pilgrimage (to employ the usual theological expression) comes to a definite end. Death brings man, as a moral and spiritual person, a kind of finality and consummation which renders his decision for or against God, reached during the time of his bodily life, final and unalterable (Denzinger 457; 464; 493a; 530f.; 693; Jn 9:4; Lk 16:26; 2 Cor 5:10). This statement, however, does not totally exclude man's further development after death, nor does it presuppose a lifeless concept of man's future life with God. The doctrine of purgatory, of the coming resurrection of the body and the future consummation of the whole universe, in fact indicates a further development of man towards his ultimate perfection in every respect. Even after the total consummation, it is of course impossible in a way to conceive the eternal life of the transfigured spirit in the immediate society of the infinite God otherwise than as a never-ending movement of the finite spirit into the life of God. But the affirmation of faith concerning the definitive ending by death of the state of pilgrimage means, as well as the survival of man's conscious personal existence, that the fundamental moral decision made by man in the mundane temporality of his bodily existence, is rendered definite and final by death. This doctrine of the faith involves taking this earthly life with radical seriousness. It is truly historical, that is, unique, unrepeatable, of inalienable and irrevocable significance. Life is suspended between a genuine beginning and a genuine end. It has a beginning, which is not one that can be resolved back into a prior constellation of reality. It begins through creation and it ends in such a way that the condition attained in freedom is not something provisional that can be superseded or changed into something indefinite or into its opposite.

There is no eternal return of all things; there is only a history, happening once and for all. There is no migration of souls for which every life is only a provisional attempt open to complete revision at a later date, which in turn, for better or for worse, may be repeated. Man does not share the incessant ebb and flow of the cycles of nature, which, in appearance at least, repeat themselves endlessly. On the contrary, it is ultimately because man is essentially a history, which happens once only, that sub-human nature also has a history: a

27

beginning through creation and a definitive end in the final transfiguration of the whole of creation before God. The history of the world and the history of the spiritual, personal individual, time with its change and alteration, is certainly not a reflection of the eternal and of its eternal yet living endlessness because it reproduces itself, endlessly unfinished, indefinitely, in instants, each of which is equally significant and equally indifferent because essentially subject to revision. Time is a unique process posited in its beginning by God's free timeless act of creation and dependent, throughout its course, on that creative act; it moves in a definite way, though one hidden from us temporal beings, towards a perfectly determined, final and irrevocable end, in which the whole of reality, each creature according to its kind, will, in a way that we cannot more precisely conceive, participate in a created way in the eternity of God. That is not a nightmare eternity, but the plenitude of reality, in absolute unity and totality, not a succession of fragmentary parts.

It is into this truly historical and Christian conception of the temporal character of the universe as moving to its immanent consummation in finite temporal succession, that the earthly life of the individual is integrated. Its historical temporal sequence moves simply between its inception and its biological death. Through this death, man in principle attains his final condition. Death for him is neither the end of his existence, nor is it a mere passage from one form of existence to another, which continues to share with the preceding its essential characteristic of indefinite temporal sequence. Death is the beginning of eternity, if and so far as we may use the term "beginning" at all in regard to this eternity. The total, created reality of the world grows in and through incarnate spiritual persons and the world is, in a certain sense, the body of those persons. Their death slowly brings the universe to its own final stage. This immanent maturing of the world toward its consummation, like that of the individual human being, is, at the same time, in a mysterious dialectical unity, a rupture, an ending from without, through an unpredictable intervention of God through his coming in judgment, no one knows the day.

The attempt more precisely to specify this doctrine of faith gives rise to a question on which Catholic theologians are not in agreement, despite its importance for a clearer grasp of the nature of death itself. The problem is whether the definitive character of the freely produced expression of man's personal existence is an intrinsic, essential constituent of death or whether it is merely linked with death (though meaningfully) by God's free decree, although death of itself would not necessarily involve such complete finality for man? To speak more concretely: does God turn death into judgment because man himself in and through his death determines his own final condition, or does judgment follow death, because God has so ordained that it is this judgment, different in itself from death, and the final happiness or unhappiness bestowed by God in this judgment, which brings about the finality of the personal attitude which death by itself could not produce?

This problem is theologically important also because it coincides with another. Is the definitive rejection by God in the judgment final because man himself in death makes his repudiation of God final, or does and can the person who is in definitive perdition not wish to return to God because God has definitively rejected him? It seems to us – and this is an opinion which can be traced to St. John Damascene and which has the weighty support of St. Thomas – that the finality of the personal life-decision is an intrinsic constituent of death itself as a spiritual and personal act of man. And if we here assume this thesis on theological grounds, which cannot be gone into more fully, the thesis would have its justification and basis even if a metaphysical analysis of the end of an incarnate spiritual person could not strictly establish its validity. One thing is, however, presupposed by this view. For if the statement that death of its very nature is a personal self-fulfilment ("one's own death" as Rilke called it) is rightly to stand, then death cannot merely be an occurrence which is passively undergone (though it clearly is that), and a biological event which man as a person faces powerlessly from the outside, but it must also be understood as an act that a man interiorly performs. Moreover, rightly understood, it must be death itself which is the act, and not simply an attitude the human being adopts towards death but which remains extrinsic to it.

Just as man is both spirit and matter, liberty and necessity, person and nature, his death too must exhibit this real, ontological dialectic, so intrinsic and essential to him. If death is the end for the whole man, that is, if through death the whole man arrives at the end of that temporal existence which is characteristic of human life and which finds its termination precisely in death, then this end must have its impact upon the whole man, the soul included. Not, obviously, in the sense that the soul ceases to exist, but in the sense suggested above, that in death the soul achieves the consummation of its own personal self-affirmation, not merely by passively suffering something which supervenes biologically, but through its own personal act. Death, therefore, as the end of man as a spiritual person, must be an active consummation from within brought about by the person himself, a maturing self-realization which embodies the result of what man has made of himself during life, the achievement of total self-possession, a real effectuation of self, the fullness of freely produced personal reality. At the same time, death as the end of the biological life is simultaneously and in a way which affects the whole man, an irruption from without, a destruction, the intervention of the Fates, an external event that turns up unexpectedly, so that a man's own death, from within, through the act of the person, is at the same time an event of the most radical spoliation of man, activity and passivity at once. If the substantial unity of man is taken really seriously, it is impossible to parcel out these two dimensions of human death, one to the body and one to the soul, thereby dissolving its very essence. What this real ontological unity of action and suffering, of active consummation of the self from within and passive submission to destruction from without, which both directly belong to the phenomenon of death, actually mean for man, will appear later.

II

DEATH AS THE CONSEQUENCE OF SIN

Man is the strange yet intimate union of personal, free spirit and matter. His death, consequently — and this was the most important conclusion reached in the first part of our essay — is both an end and a fulfilment. His temporal bodily life is ended by the separation of body and soul; in the same process, his personal fulfilment, in which he brings the total result of his life's activity to its final state, is achieved from within. In the sources of faith, death is described as the separation of body and soul, in so far as it is the end of bodily life striking man from without, and as the end of our pilgrimage on earth, in so far as it is a personal consummation. A more exact interpretation of the expression "separation of body and soul", made it clear that this phrase is not to be interpreted as meaning that man's spiritual reality is taken completely out of the world. This separation results rather in an opening of the soul to a new relationship with the world in its inner unity, one which is no longer mediated by a body with space-time limitations. But, even though this may not have been particularly emphasized, the intimate connection and correlation of those two basic statements about death also became clearer. Since such an intrinsic relationship of the personal principle in man remains and even attains its full perfection in death, it is easier to understand that the total achievement of a human life, which even in its spiritual-personal character was accomplished in the material world, is preserved in death and will eventually again find expression in concrete bodily form in the resurrection of the body. That was, approximately, the result of the first part of our considerations.

Our method, as before, will not be to develop further insight into the nature of death out of one basic speculative idea, but to start from a direct statement explicitly contained in the Church's teaching. After the statements about the universality of death, about the separation of body and soul and about death as the end of man's pilgrimage, we shall now explore a fourth statement: death is a consequence of sin. This truth must now be considered: our death, as the death of Adam, as the death of the sinner.

The immediate background of this fourth proposition is clear: death, as it is in fact suffered individually and universally by men, in the present economy of salvation stands in causal relation to sin, above all to the sin committed by the head and progenitor of the whole human race in his rôle as head. The original human being, according to the testimony of Scripture, was created with the possibility of not dying. Man, in the actual concrete order, dies because he lost original justice in the first man, the one head and progenitor, by this first man's free rejection of God. Original justice consisted in a union with God through grace which transformed man's whole spiritual being, penetrating even his bodily life. Consequently

33

actual death is a visible expression of the disharmony between God and man in man's very being which supervened at the beginning of his spiritual and moral history. Because man has lost the divine life in union with God by grace, his earthly existence also disintegrates. Man's subjection to death is the manifestation of his disharmony with God. Our task now is to consider this statement of faith, and patiently, step by step, to interpret its more exact meaning and the problems it raises.

1. Adam's Freedom from Death

If death is the consequence of the fall of the first man, this implies that, before his sin, the first man was not under the necessity of dying. This doctrine of faith of course does not mean that the first man in Paradise, had he not sinned, would have lived on endlessly in the bodily life of this world. It can confidently be said that he would surely have had an end to his life; remaining in his bodily constitution of course, he would have brought this life of his from within to its perfect and full maturity. In other words, Adam would have brought his personal life to its perfect consummation even in his bodily form through a "death" which would have been a pure, active self-affirmation, attaining a perfection of an embodied kind yet open to the world in its totality, the perfection we now look for as the final result of the redemption, and as the eschatological miracle of the resurrection of the body. This end of man in Paradise, this "death" without dying, would have been a pure apparent and active consummation of the whole man from within, without death in the proper sense, that is, without suffering from without any violent dissolution of the actual bodily constitution. This insight is significant not only in reference to the lot of man in Paradise which has ceased to have any reality, but also because it draws our attention to the fact that not every aspect of our death can be considered a consequence of sin that ought not to have been.

2. Death as Guilt and as a Natural Phenomenon

When we reflect that man in Paradise, even before his sin and his falling away from God, would have consummated his life on this earth; when, further, we recall that a finality and a consummation of this life, even after the fall, still takes place through what we now experience as our death, we can recognize that death evidently cannot be merely a consequence of man's empty and meaningless guilt. It was noted earlier in passing, that the proposition of faith which places the historical origin of death in human guilt, does not prejudge the question whether and to what extent on the basis of our empirical knowledge of man, it might be established that death is a natural consequence of human nature, and, if this is the case, must like all natural events bear a positive intrinsic meaning. It is, in fact, a doctrine of faith that death considered in itself is also a natural event, as an immediate consequence of the constitution of man as body and spirit. When discussing earlier the universality of death, the question was left undecided whether the statement that death is a natural event, can be demonstrated by a purely human natural science or by a metaphysical anthropology. At all events even if this were not possible,

35

and it is not really as easy as it might perhaps appear from the materially composite character of the body and from the union of body and soul, Catholic theology, as against the Protestant reformers and the Jansenists, holds on theological grounds that death is also a natural event; or, to state it more cautiously, that the death which we actually do experience has also a natural essence. The decisive theological reason, to omit others, is that death must be not only a consequence, an expression, and a punishment for sin, but also, as will be explained in more detail later, a dying with Christ, the participation in, and appropriation of, his redemptive death. Since death is also to be the very opposite of sin, and since it cannot be both the consequence of sin and a dying with Christ at the same time (in the sense of a paradox of dialectical theology in which sin and grace, despair and hope, judgment and mercy are ultimately and necessarily always the same), then death must have a natural essence proper to it. It may be either of the two possibilities; which it is, is finally determined by the way in which a man, as a person, sustains this feature of his nature. Only then (since this attitude of man is itself an intrinsic factor of death) does it become the whole which is called death. There must be in death, as it is an actual event for each individual, some common element, neutral, so to speak, which permits us to say that, in a true sense, all men die the same death (although death as it afflicts each individual actually is indeed salvation or damnation, and although "same" as used in this context cannot refer to death taken in its comprehensive meaning). As a consequence, objectively, we can never know which death each individual dies in fact, the death of Adam or the death of Christ.

Here theology itself demands an ontology of death; because for the reason already indicated the death which is actually experienced by all men individually cannot be identified quite simply from the start with that natural essence of death which we postulate. Even if, when considering actual death, we disregard the radically different attitudes of those who endure it (though these attitudes belong, strictly speaking, to the reality of death), the phenomenon which remains, that is, the end of this life and the dissolution of the bodily constitution, is still not identical with the natural essence of death. For the phenomenon of natural death, which does exist, does not accord logically and without difficulties with the actual constitution of man in the supernatural order. In the concrete order, man, whether in the state of grace or not, lives in an order in which death should not exist. In the orientation towards grace and the supernatural goal of sharing in the life of God, there is in every human being a real ontological feature which contradicts death. And so, quite apart from whether. this can be brought to consciousness by simple reflection or not, the individual in the concrete can experience death, for all its natural character, and even prior to the attitude in which he endures it, as a goal inwardly striven for, not as a matter of course belonging to the immanent destiny of his "nature". Consequently, this Catholic doctrine concerning the natural element in death does not mean that the actual death which each of us will die may be looked upon as a natural process, as though death could be neutralized, so to speak, and rendered irrelevant to man's spiritual, supernatural existence in the order of grace, as is commonly urged against this Catholic doctrine by Protestants. In addition, death is in fact an event of nation. We shall have to recall a number of points to which reference has already been made. Death appears to simple experience to be the end of the whole man. Not, of course, in the sense that man simply ceases to exist, or that the "soul" ceases absolutely to exist and all that remains is what is still open to empirical inspection, i. e. the corpse. Such an interpretation of death as an end would proceed on the supposition that what no longer falls under the observation of the senses no longer exists at all. This assumption is without logical grounds and for many reasons (which we cannot and do not need to discuss here) absolutely unacceptable in the present case, for the spiritual, simple and personal principle in man, his soul, for ethical as well as for ontological reasons, can and must continue to exist. But death appears to our experience to be an end in the sense that for the whole of man there somehow comes an end of that temporal character which is characteristic of human life. This statement is valid for the soul too, at least to the extent that death appears as a phenomenon not simply of the body but of the whole man, who in experience always figures as a unity, and that there is no actual concrete reason to except the soul, because it survives after death, from this completion of the human being in his unity whose moment has come. "End" is a varying, highly analogous concept; on differing levels of existence and activity it cannot but have a different character, according to the particular constitution and diverse potentialities of different things. It would be ontologically mistaken and false to refer a concept of "end" proper to one level of existence to another level. If it were possible in the present context to offer, on the basis of a metaphysical anthropology, an ontology of this concept of "end" which

39

would exhibit its analogical variability as well as the specific character of the human level of existence, the following conclusions concerning the special character of the human end, death, might well emerge. The end of man, considered only from man's point of view, presents in inseparable and irreducible unity an ontologically dialectical opposition of elements. The end of man as a spiritual person is an active fulfilment from within, an act of self-completion, a life-synthesizing self-affirmation, a person's total taking possession of himself, the final act of self-formation, the plenitude of personal reality. At the same time, inseparably and in a way which affects the whole human being, the death of man as the end of a material biological being is a destruction, a rupture, an accident which strikes man from without, unforeseeably, with no assurance that it will strike him at the moment in which interiorly he has completed his life. Death is a blow of fate, a thief in the night, an emptying and reducing of man to powerlessness, in fact, the end. This simultaneity of fulfilment and emptiness, of actively achieved and passively suffered end, of full self-possession and of being completely dispossessed of self, may, for the moment, be taken as a correct description of the phenomenon we call death.

The suppression of one or other aspect of death would result in error either in the material or spiritual direction, either debasing man's death to the level of the animal although he is a spiritual person, or leaving the personality of man unaffected by death, although he is a natural being. At this point of our analysis of the phenomenon of death, it may be well to emphasize again that our problem is not whether man does or does not continue to exist after death. We can take it for granted here that he does. The problem is rather how he continues to exist after death and how the answer to this question may perhaps emerge from an analysis of the phenomenon of death itself. At this point we encounter that irreducible dialectical unity of death which we want to call its obscure, hidden character. Death appears both as act and fate, as end and fulfilment, as willed and as suffered, as plenitude and emptiness. It seems to involve an empty, unsubstantial uncanny character, a kind of de-personalization, loss of self, destruction, and at the same time the plenitude of a person's attainment of total self-possession, the independence and pure immanence that characterize personality. Yet both these sets of aspects belong to the phenomenon of death. It will never really be possible, therefore, humanly speaking, to say with certainty in the concrete case whether or not the decisive immanent self-realization which must belong to death as the end of a spiritual person, is an experience of ultimate futility; whether the highest act, by which man completely disposes of himself, is an absolute abandonment of self; whether in fact in view of the finality of man's moral decision which comes with death, and the passing away of mere appearance and the coming to light of what really belongs to man's genuine nature, it is the manifestation of supreme and final wickedness, and therefore of man's radical futility. It is not possible to say whether the full term of life reached in death is not in fact the emptiness and futility which till then was concealed, or, conversely, whether the emptiness apparent in death is only the outward aspect of a true plenitude, deceptive only to us who are not dead. In other words it is not possible to say whether the end of an intrinsically temporal existence and the surrender of a

41

guisedly and tangibly experienced. The fact that man since Adam brings to accomplishment the death which is his act, in the empty finality of the death which he undergoes, so that death as a human act is obscured by death as suffering, visibly manifests the absence of divine grace. Death, therefore, is the penalty of sin.

In this way, however, death can not only be the penal consequence of sin, but also the culmination of sin itself, mortal sin in the strictest sense of the word. Since death is hidden in darkness, the concrete and final interpretation of this hidden situation can, if man is acting rightly, come to him only from God. On account of its obscurity, man should and ought to understand the concrete existential situation of death, in so far as it is his own deed, as the culmination of that anticipatory attitude (a prefiguration of faith) in which man surrenders himself and what he is in unconditional openness to the disposition of the incomprehensible God, without presuming to know what that sovereign liberty of God may, in this obscure and therefore for him not entirely comprehensible death, decide concerning him. This in turn makes it possible to understand how death can be a mortal sin. We have already noted that for theological reasons death cannot be conceived merely as something passively suffered, a destruction coming from without, but must also be conceived as an act of man, coming from within.

Clearly it cannot be an act of man, if it is conceived as an isolated point at the end of life, but only if it is understood as an act of fulfilment (a concept which an ontology of the end of a spiritual being can fully justify), achieved through the act of the whole of life in such a manner that death is

43

axiologically present all through human life. Man is enacting his death, as his own consummation, through the deed of his life, and in this way death is present in his actions, that is, in each of his free acts, in which he freely disposes of his whole person. Consequently, the death present in these acts of life explicitly or implicitly, can be mortal sin. In order to try to point out even briefly how man may make a mortal sin of the deed of his life, it can only be a question of indicating how he can, more or less explicitly, understand and enact his death sinfully all through his life, and not merely at its end. There can be no question of showing how each mortal sin, implicitly and tacitly also includes a false and sinful understanding of death.

We have already suggested that death, because of its darkness, is faced rightly when it is entered upon by man as an act in which he surrenders himself fully and with unconditional openness to the disposal of the incomprehensible decision of God, because, in the darkness of death, man is not in a position to dispose of himself unambiguously. Conversely, we can also say that mortal sin consists in the will to die autonomously, when death's open orientation towards God (which is contained in its obscurity) is not consented to, and by this refusal a man does not give himself up to the disposition of God, according to which death is a penalty of original sin and a sharing in Christ's redemptive death, and which is expressed in grace and the supernatural framework within which all human life is set. In more concrete terms, the sinful understanding of death in the activity of life can be related either directly and explicitly to the open character of human death precisely as a natural phenomenon, or to the two essential components of man, body and soul, the specific ontological dialectic of which reaches its highest and final tension in death. In the first case, man denies explicitly and concretely the radically problematic and questionable character of death as something hidden. This again may happen in two ways. The denial may be enacted in despair; the obscure character of death which puts man's whole being in question, is conceived as something absolute, because man, relying on himself, does not see any chance of unveiling death's dark mystery, and is unwilling to seek help in doing so from any other source. Or man may simply deny that death is obscure and problematic at all, and try to interpret the definitive meaning of his death positively and independently, by a concrete grasp of his own nature. This kind of sinful attempt at an autonomous interpretation of death leads inevitably to the second mode of denial. In this, the autonomous interpretation of death denies its obscure character, and the dialectic between the two essential constituent parts of man, on which that obscure character is based, is contested in favour of one or the other of these principles. Consequently, in this second case also, two kinds of sinful understanding of death are possible. There is, first, the possibility of a spiritualist aberration. Through death, the spiritual principle in man is considered to be freed from the confines of matter and corporeal existence, and by virtue of man's nature alone death means transformation to the state of free spirit. We need not inquire further here how this free, spiritual existence is then conceived. It may be regarded as in some way still an individual mode of existence, or thought of as absorption into a universal spirit, imagined to be a moral subject untouched by death, a subjec-

4. Death as a Penalty for Original Sin

Death, it was said above, is a penalty for sin. This statement must be more precisely explained and the theological problems arising from it must at least be indicated. The death which men after Adam must die, we noted, has an obscure, hidden character and this makes it possible for death to be an event of salvation or of damnation. It may be a darkness which manifests eternal death, or it may be the twilight, in which alone the faith is possible by which man appropriates the salvation effected by Christ. In order to understand this, the following must be considered. The obscure character of death is an element proper to death itself. It belongs to death as a natural process, deriving from its nature, from its very constitution as the death of a being both spiritual and corporeal. If death is to appear as a punishment of sin, and if this penalty cannot consist solely in the loss of a good which is indeed one and can be known to be such, but the disappearance of which cannot be concretely experienced as an actual loss, because, being a "supernatural" gift, it cannot in fact be experienced on the purely natural plane as a concrete object of desire, then Adam's exemption from death, which is now abrogated, must despite its unmerited and supernatural character, represent some kind of "need" or "requirement". It is this that causes the loss of Adam's immunity from death to be experienced as contrary to the concrete dynamic tendency of man as he actually is, and so gives it the character of a punishment. Now this is in fact the case.* After Adam's fall,

* Cf. my essays: "Concerning the Relationship between Nature and Grace" in *Theological Investigations* I (London 1961), 297—317; and "Über

man was never pure nature, capable of understanding and fulfilling himself on his own, once the supernatural vocation to sharing the life of God was gone. After the Fall, man still has that vocation as an obligation and task, as a real feature characterizing what he is, as a component constitutive of the supernatural setting of human life. And in that supernatural setting (because the original gift of immortality was a connatural consequence of supernatural grace), there is included a tendency to that perfection of man which would have made of his end a pure and experienced maturation from within. When man in this supernatural setting dies a death which is obscure and hidden in character, which overwhelms him from without and dispossesses him utterly, he is dying a death which even now really ought not to be. He is experiencing a death, the darkness of which is an expression and consequence and punishment of the perdition which ensues for him from Adam's sin, even if he is not able clearly to realize this.

The following question may serve to make what we mean more precise. Does death, as the penalty for original sin, in some way represent a fresh, retributive intervention on the part of God, imposing a penalty not intrinsically related to the sin itself, or is death the expression of that sin, flowing immediately from its very essence? In other words: is death a punishment because it is a consequence and manifestation of sin in the corporeal life of man, or, on the contrary, is it an expression and manifestation of sin because it is sin's punishment? We can offer only a brief reply. A closer interpretation, based on St. Thomas, of the grace with which our

das Verhältnis des Naturgesetzes zur übernatürlichen Gnadenordnung" in *Orientierung* 20 (1956), 8—11.

first parents were endowed, and to which the gift of immortality belonged as a connatural consequence of the divinization of man by grace in his paradisal state, would indicate, it would seem, that death is primarily an expression and manifestation of the essence of sin in the bodily constitution of man, and as such, as a consequence, a punishment for sin. Death is the expression of the fact that the earthly reality of man is no longer or not yet completely permeated and transformed by grace, of the fact that grace must begin again so radically as it were the activity by which it transforms that earthly reality, that grace cannot at once completely eliminate death and transcend it by a purely transfiguring fulfilment of man. Because this relationship between the earthly reality of man and grace, which finds expression and culminates in the darkness of death, "really" ought not to be, since it came about only through man's original sin and contradicts his supernatural destiny, death also expresses this relationship and hence is a punishment for sin. It is a punishment because it is a consequence and a connatural expression of the situation which was brought about by original sin. Death is guilt made visible.

These reflections also illustrate the relationship between death and concupiscence, or unruly desire, which is another expression and another punishment of man's alienation from God by original sin. Concupiscence, as a consequence of original sin, is nothing else than the antagonism between nature and the person endowed with grace or at least with a supernatural destiny. It implies that the divine life is in some way impeded by man's earthly reality, which does not allow this divine life purely and perfectly to penetrate and transform the whole reality of man, even his body and its instincts.

On that basis it is easy to understand that the law of death, which implies the impossibility of integrating and bringing to immediate and visible expression the grace-given perfection of man in a perfected body too, is nothing else than the clearest expression of concupiscence in its character of original sin's consequence. Death is the culmination of concupiscence; concupiscence manifests the continuous presence of death, which spreads its veil of darkness over human fulfilment all through life.

5. Death as Personal Mortal Sin

Death is not only the expression and visible mark of man's alienation from God, of his lot since Adam's fall; it is also, as a more careful examination of the doctrine of the New Testament on death (Rom 1:32; 7:9–10; 8:13; 6:16, 21, 23; 7:5; 8:2; James 1:15; and also St. John) will incline one to admit, a consequence of grave, personal (and unforgiven) sins. As in the case of original sin, so here, too, death is an intrinsic, essential expression and visible manifestation of these personal sins in the entire reality of man, body and soul. That this statement does not contradict the fact that the justified and holy people who are without personal grievous sin also die, should be clear from what has already been said. For death, as we have noted, is not a mere accident, suffered passively, striking all men, sinner and just alike, in the same manner and quality; it is also an active consummation, worked out through the whole of life, and, therefore, it is an act of man. As a consequence, it is different for the just and for the sinner even when the external event, which in everyday life we call death, seems to be the same. Beneath the veil of darkness the very centre of the phenomenon of death can differ profoundly from case to case.

The assertion that death is also an expression and penal consequence of personal sins is confirmed by St. Paul's doctrine that there is a connection between God's law without grace, and death. He refers to the conditions under which the divine law, without the grace of Christ, becomes in fact (though against its proper, original and intrinsic intention) the occasion of sin (1 Cor 15:56) and under which the law itself, by stirring up the sinful protest of man against it, provokes death as the consequence of this sin and brings death about; and not the death of the soul alone, but death which includes the end of the bodily life of man in the way we experience it (2 Cor 3:6; Rom 7:5, 10, 13).

6. Death and the Devil

Another point within the scope of the problem of sin and death which demands careful consideration is the relationship between sinful death and the devil. This relationship is referred to in the Bible (Heb 2:14; Jn 8:44; Wis 2:24; Gen 31; cf. Denzinger 788). Because death is a consequence of sin, it appears in Scripture as an expression of the realm of Satan as ruler of this world. Satan's lordship over death, as clearly stated in the Bible, is based, first of all, on the fact that Adam's sin, which brought death into the world, was occasioned by the devil's temptation. Of itself, this connection does not, it would seem, offer an adequate explanation of the relationship between death and the devil. Two problems in particular

51

suggest themselves. First it may be asked whether death in the sub-human world is an expression of a fall of the whole of creation in the fall of the angels. This question must be left undecided in the present context; an adequate answer would call for a more exact study of the general and basic relationship of the pure spirits to the material world and of the possible implications for the material creation of the glorification by divine grace of the whole angelic world. Such a study, obviously, lies beyond the scope the present essay.

The second question is whether the relationship between human death and the devil is the result of the single historical event of the first man's temptation by the snake, which drove Adam into sin and brought death into the world, or whether there is also here a more intimate relationship between the demonic power of Satan and the death of the individual man, at least in its character as a sinful death? That such a direct relation does exist may readily be assumed, if it is true, on the one hand, that personal sins find their retributive expression in death and, on the other, if it can be assumed that any grave sin on a man's part is associated in some way with demonic temptation. Furthermore, the relationship between the devil and death can be grasped even more fundamentally if we assume, as was briefly mentioned in the first part of this essay, that the angels, notwithstanding, and indeed because of, their constitution as pure spirits, have a fundamental relationship to the visible world, springing from their very nature, and consequently, that their influence on that world is not sporadic, deriving from their own decision.

Assuming this fundamental, though non-corporeal, and hence pancosmic relationship of an essential kind between the angels and the world, it will then have to be said that the angel wills the perfection of the world, because that reflects his own perfection and expresses it. To the extent that death means not only a termination, an end, but a consummation as well, the angel must will death in the world; and in the full accomplishment of his own nature there is included a dynamic principle which drives the world towards this consummation in death. As long as the angels remained in grace, their grace-endowed nature could only express itself in the world in that pure consummation which would have characterized the death-transcending end of man in Paradise. If all the angels had remained in grace, the world, too, would have been above death. The fallen angel, however, wills the perfection of his essence in proud autonomy, without grace; consequently, he must will the perfection of the universe without grace. Since death is that terminating consummation of the world (of incarnate spirit), which can be overcome only through the grace of a pure, unveiled consummation, the fallen angel must will death as such, for death is the perfect expression of the devil's will for a consummation without grace of his own essence and of the world. This expression of the angel's freely and sinfully achieved consummation of his nature can become a reality for man only through man's free consent, in his quality as a free, spiritual being endowed with grace. By this consent, man wills his own graceless, autonomous fulfilment. Therefore, the will of the fallen angel for his own perfection and its expression in the world is *eo ipso* a temptation of man to a similar autonomous fulfilment without grace and so a temptation to death, everywhere and always when such a human decision is in

53

question. The relationship of the angels to the world in general is that of lordship; the same, consequently, is true of their relation to death. The dominion of the angels is expressed in death; here their quality and status as the graceless lords and principalities of the universe is manifested. The devil, according to Hebrews 2:14, is one who possesses the power of death.

Death is absolutely universal. Everyone declares it natural and obvious that he must die. Yet a secret protest and an inextinguishable horror of this end abides in every man. A metaphysical anthropology cannot explain this fact. If it recognizes that man as a spiritual being is immortal, it is not really possible to understand why he should be so afraid to die. Unless of course man's fear of death is reduced to a mere expression of the purely vital, bodily urge of self-preservation, which simply falsifies the problem. Dogma and theology intervene at this point. Man is, rightly, afraid of death. Actually, he should not die, for he still possesses within himself, either in reality, or as a requirement that he has to meet, that vitality of divine life, which if it could assert itself pure and unveiled in this earthly life, would completely eliminate death.

That man dies, and does not simply come to completion, is a consequence of the sin at the beginning of human history and of all the sins through which every man makes his own the sin of his first parent. This consequence is not merely a punishment imposed by God, striking man, so to say, from without, and exhibiting no intrinsic relationship to the offence punished. Death as suffering and destruction coming from without, like the thief in the night (which it will always be) is, obviously, subject to the free disposition of God's will. It will always, therefore, include the character of a divine judgment among its notes. But it is sin that is manifested in death. The emptiness, hopelessness, the transitoriness, indeterminateness, the inextricable confusion of noblest action and most humiliating passivity, of plain meaning and ultimate ambiguity, all these characteristics of the death which we must actually die are nothing but the manifestations of sin, to which in some higher and hidden dimension these characteristics analogically belong. Because a creature belongs to God, it shrinks back, by a movement of its very essence, from this last mystery of emptiness, of finality, of nothingness, from the mystery of iniquity. Because this same creature, whether holy or sinful, is driven as long as he lives by the power of the divine life which calls him and works in him, he will always experience a mysterious horror of death, which can never be explained by himself, or from what he can observe in himself. In this horror of death, there emerges on the visible surface of human life, the horror of that death which alone is true death. If men try effectively to hide the reality of this horror from themselves by explaining it away by their manner of life, by taking refuge either in frivolity, despair or a tragic heroism, then by this very act they make of it what they will not admit terrifies them in it, the beginning of eternal death. Death and man's attitude towards it, which of course is really a part of its very nature, is not abolished or extinguished but is permanently transformed only when in the light and power of Jesus Christ who died and rose again, it is seen and borne as what it can be, the darkness of that night of the Cross in which eternal life penetrated in death the very depths of the world, in order to give life to the world. But that is the subject of the next part.

55

manner in which in death the process of appropriation of the redemptive power of Christ's death receives its sacramental visibility in Christ's sacraments.

1. The Death of Christ

The Word of God, through the incarnation in the womb of the Virgin, and, consequently, of our race, became of the same nature as we. It follows that, in a real sense, Christ died our death, the death of the human race fallen in Adam, though of course this does not mean that his death was absolutely like ours in every respect. But if he really became like us in everything but sin, as the Epistle to the Hebrews says, then he became like us in death, too, and his death cannot be similar to ours merely in externals. When Scripture and the Creed confess that he died, the meaning of this extends far beyond what may be observed through human empirical knowledge of the historical event which happened under Pontius Pilate. This is demonstrated at once, for instance, by the fact that Scripture adds as an intrinsic factor to the affirmation of his death, the further assertion of his descent into the lower world. This establishes the essential similarity of Christ's death with our own; for that descent into hell is considered, not simply as an redemptive activity performed after Christ's death (Acts 2: 24, 31) but as an essential factor in his death; and this accords with both Old and New Testament, for such a descent into hell was regarded as an essential element in human death, at least according to the situation in the economy of salvation then prevailing.

We have already seen that death is many-sided: action and suffering, a surrender of the bodily form and the opening out of a pancosmic relation of the spirit, an end of the historical life on a biological basis and the consummation of the personal life from within. Even if Scripture in speaking of the death of Jesus places no emphasis on these different dimensions, we should still expect that his death, being of the same nature as our own, would exhibit a similar complexity. We know that his death means our redemption; it is not yet clear, however, on which of the many dimensions of death that redemption is based. At least from the point of view of method, we have to entertain the possibility that redemption rests on no single feature of Christ's death, but upon that death taken as whole, embracing all its manifold factors.

Methodical considerations, moreover, make it difficult to accept with complete satisfaction the theory of redemption as it was worked out in the early Middle Ages and as it has, with but slight modifications, been taught ever since. That theory, we may hold, did not capture in its concepts the full reality of the redemption as recounted, explicitly or implicitly, in Scripture, although we can, and indeed must, accept as well-founded the positive content of the theory. The theory to which we refer is the so-called theory of satisfaction, according to which the moral acts of Christ, in consequence of the infinite dignity of his divine person, are of infinite value in spite of the fact that these acts in themselves, as acts of his human, spiritual and free nature, are ontologically finite. Since the gravity of the offence and of the disrespect is measured by the dignity of the person offended and not by that of the offender, the sin of a free creature is an infinite offence because it is directed against the majesty of God, and cannot be repaired by the satisfaction of a mere creature. For the moral value of the satisfaction, in turn, is determined by the personal dignity, not of the person offended, but of the person who offers the satisfaction.

On the supposition that God is disposed to forgive man's guilt and restore the lost grace of divine life only in view of full reparation for the sin committed, which is infinite, being directed against God, only the incarnate Word of God, in his human nature, is capable of offering due satisfaction for us in virtue of his personal dignity. However, since the mission of the eternal Word into our human life precedes the satisfaction Christ offers for sin, and is not dependent on it, the redeeming will of God, his readiness to restore grace to men, is, in spite of the satisfaction offered by Christ, a pure work of divine favour and mercy. The moral work upon the performance of which God willed the restitution of grace to man to depend, was the free acceptance of death by Christ. In this view it was the free disposition of God that determined that it was to be precisely this obedience to death that had to be shown. Since any other moral act of Christ in his human nature, because of the dignity of his divine person, would also possess infinite value, it would have been just as possible, on this theory, for God to have prescribed and accepted any other moral act of Christ as the satisfaction required.

The positive content of this theory of satisfaction is, without doubt, true. In its core, it is justified by the very fact that Scripture, too, sees the redeeming act of Christ in his obedience, his love, in his free acceptance of death. It remains questionable, however, whether this concept of satisfaction does adequately express the full reality of Christ's redemptive death. For it does not make it intrinsically clear why it was through Christ's death that we were redeemed, and not through some other possible act of our Lord, which would also have been of infinite value. To refer to the free disposition of God (though no one could contest the ultimate correctness of this answer) seems perhaps rather premature. Certainly Scripture sees Christ's death as an act of his obedience, of his humiliation, and of his love. At the same time, it emphasizes as much, if not more, that it was precisely through his death that Christ redeemed us, and it is plain that Scripture sees his death as something more than just any act of his obedience and his love (chosen, as it were, by the arbitrary will of God), equal with other acts of Christ, as if death possessed no specific character decisive for our redemption. On the contrary, it must be recognized that Scripture obviously considers this death as redemptive precisely under the characteristics which are proper to death alone and not to any other moral act. It asserts that we were freed and redeemed precisely through the blood which Christ shed for us and through his body which was given for us and it insists that the redeeming act was a bloody sacrifice in the ritual sense, which essentially presupposes the death of the victim and, finally, as we see more clearly in Tradition, a transformation and reconciliation of the whole world is brought about through Christ's death. The efficacy of Christ's death consequently cannot be attributed to it as directly as this in its general quality as a moral act but only in its precise character as death. The theory of satisfaction, however, leaves open precisely why we were redeemed through Christ's death. The positive content of the theory may, therefore, be used as a stepping-stone; but we must go beyond it if in order to solve the problem we must take into account factors belonging to death as such which render it absolutely different from any other possible event of human life and activity.

The satisfaction theory falls short on another point, for it takes for granted from the start that death, as such, is purely passive, an occurrence passively undergone, distinct from human activity. On this tacit but in reality questionable assumption, the redeeming act of Christ will not reside in his death as such, but only in his patient and obedient submission to the suffering which caused his death, and this does not do justice to the statements of Scripture.

We can offer here only a slight positive complement to the satisfaction theory, chiefly applying the insight previously attained into the essence of death. As Christ became man of the fallen race of Adam, and assumed the "flesh of sin", he entered human life in a situation in which that life reaches its fulfilment only by passing through death in all its obscurity. That is, he took death upon himself inasmuch as in the actual order of things it is an expression and manifestation of the fallen state of creation in both angels and in man. Even though Christ was not in a state of belief, he nevertheless experienced in himself the darkness which is the specific character of human death and the deprivation of the personal consummation in the void of the bodily end. He not only offered a satisfaction of some kind for sin, but he enacted and suffered precisely the death which is the expression, manifestation and revelation of sin in the world. He did all this in absolute liberty, as the act and the revelation of that divine grace which divinized the life of his humanity and which, by reason of his own divine person, belonged to him of natural necessity. In that way however, death became, at least for himself, something absolutely different from what it would be in a man who did not possess, in his own right, either the life of grace, or that absolute freedom, secure from all the weakness of concupiscence, which was properly Christ's. It is precisely in its darkness that the death of Christ becomes the expression and embodiment of his loving obedience, the free transference of his entire created existence to God. What was the manifestation of sin, thus becomes, without its darkness being lifted, the contradiction of sin, the manifestation of a "yes" to the will of the Father. The precise meaning of this statement may perhaps more appropriately be discussed in the context of our consideration of Christian death as the culminating appropriation of redemption. What will be said there, granted the necessary modifications, will apply to Christ's human enactment and suffering of death. Naturally, there is an essential difference between him and us. He performed all this in virtue of a grace necessarily his due as a divine person, while the grace which helps us to endure our death, is his grace. Still this does not destroy the intrinsic similarity between Christ and ourselves in enduring death, for his death, too, is obedience and love. Only one or two things can be indicated here. Man's death, in so far as it is his own personal act, extends through his whole life. If this is so, it makes it easier to comprehend how the life and death of Christ in their redemptive significance also form a unity. His life redeems, inasmuch as his death is axiologically present in his entire life. And in so far as any moral act of man is to be considered as a disposing over his entire person with regard to his interior destiny, and in so far as such a disposition receives its final character only in death, it is clear (on the supposition that Christ assumed the flesh of sin and death) that we cannot really say that Christ could have redeemed us through any other moral act than his death, even had God been disposed to accept some other act. Therefore, it is just as correct to say that his obedience is redemption, because it is death, as it is to say that his death effects our redemption, because it is obedience.

But in all this little is really said about Christ's death considered in itself. The question why his death is redemption for us others, and what can be said by the theology of death on this to complete the usual satisfaction theory, is still left unanswered. We have already remarked that it is in death, and only in death, that man enters into an open, unrestricted relationship to the cosmos as a whole, that he is integrated, as a constant and determining factor, into the world as a whole, through his own total reality achieved in his life and death. In other words, because death in some way opens to man the real ontological relationship of his soul to the world as a whole, it is through his death that man in some way introduces as his contribution the result of his life into the radical, real ground of the unity of the world. Applying this hypothesis of the metaphysical anthropology of death to the death of Christ, we must say that through Christ's death, his spiritual reality, which he possessed from the beginning, enacted in his life, and brought to consummation in his death, becomes open to the whole world and is inserted into this whole world in its ground as a permanent determination of a real ontological kind. In support of this line of speculation,

63

we might refer to the teaching of our faith that concerns Christ's descent into hell, that is, Sheol, the lower world.

We have already noted that, according to the New Testament, this descent of Christ into hell is not simply based on a soteriological act on behalf of the saved who lived before Christ and who, before his death, could not yet share in the vision of God. It is conceived rather as a feature emerging from the very essence of Christ's death, because it was a human death. The Old Testament, it is true, as well as the theology prevalent in the time of Christ, viewed the period in the lower world under a negative aspect, as implying the absence of the eschatological glorification of the body. Nevertheless, since death, as a natural phenomenon, cannot consist in something purely negative, we can also seek a positive aspect in the descent into hell even if this has remained relatively implicit. The basic images in our usual idea of hell include "depth", something "underneath", something "more inward", belonging to the "background", something "more essential" and "radically one". Thus we may suppose in general that when we think of man entering the lower world we at least implicitly think of him as establishing contact with the intrinsic, radically unified, ultimate and deepest level of the reality of the world. Consequently in the profession of our faith in the descent of Christ into hell, as it is stated in the Creed, we may perhaps implicitly include, and apply to Christ's death as well, the idea which resulted from our general consideration of death as the separation of body and soul. If we suppose, in accordance with that line of speculation, that through death Christ established an open, real ontological relationship to the world in its unity which is the ground of its spatio-temporal diversification (a relation not mediated by his body, which in death is separated from his soul, nor established subsequently and retrospectively through the reassumption of the glorified body), we may understand, in some way, why his death has more than one redemptive significance for us.

The world is not only a condition presupposed to the making of decisions by spiritual persons, the condition of the very possibility of such decisions, when it is thought of as the sum of the various individual things influencing man's decisions. Corresponding to the substantial connection of the soul with material reality, which reaches to the very depths of the latter, a non-spatial unity belongs to this aeon, and the soul by reason of the substantial unity of man is in communication with it. And in death, the soul, far from losing its relationship to that dimension, is, in fact, for the first time rendered open to it. The concrete character of that unity, therefore, is to provide a prior constitutive framework and factor which contributes to determine the possibilities of personal action in every case for everyone. The possibility of personal action is partly determined by the special quality of that radical oneness in which all things in the universe communicate with each other. Consequently, if the reality of Christ, as consummated through his death, in his death is built into this unity of the cosmos, thus becoming a feature and intrinsic principle of it, and a prior framework and factor of all personal life in the world, that means that the world as a whole and as the scene of personal human actions has become different from what it would have been had Christ not died. And so possibilities of a real ontological nature were opened up for the personal action of all other men which would not have existed without

65

the death of our Lord. By that death his human reality and grace, definitively ratified by the real concrete human freedom of his death, became a determining feature of the whole cosmos. The thought that Christ, in his life and death, belongs to the innermost reality of the world, would be less alien to us if we were not so prone to identify the world with the handful of crude and superficial data gathered from everyday sense-experience, or if we were better able to realize how profound, mysterious and filled with spiritual realities this world is, and how everyone draws life from the whole of the universe, which extends to such measureless depths. When the vessel of his body was shattered in death, Christ was poured out over all the cosmos; he became actually, in his very humanity, what he had always been by his dignity, the heart of the universe, the innermost centre of creation. Realizing this, we might better grasp the fact that we, in our spiritual lives as human persons, willingly or unwillingly, whether we accept or deny it, are always concerned with this ultimate depth of the world which was occupied by Christ when, in death, he descended into the lower world.

For confirmation of this tentative interpretation of Christ's death as the establishment of a definite situation in regard to salvation for all spiritual beings belonging to this universe in virtue of their bodily constitution, we may refer to a theological opinion which, though controverted, is nevertheless held by many theologians of great authority. This is the doctrine of the natural or physical (though not, in the sense of "physics") instrumental causality of Christ's humanity with respect to grace for all men since Christ. According to this opinion, Christ's humanity does not have a merely juridical and moral causality in regard to the grace given to man through his acts, his suffering and death; beyond this, it is immediately, even though only instrumentally, connected with the grace which God effects in man. This is substantially what we propose in our opinion. Our opinion, however, by means of the theory of the pancosmic relationship of the soul to the whole of the world attained in death, seems to us to explain more readily how Christ's humanity can enter into an effective active relationship with all men.

2. *The Death of the Christian as a Dying with Christ*

A Christian in the state of grace dies a different death from that of the sinner. Not only is the final outcome in the next life reached through death, different for each, but the death itself is different. This truth (which of course is always present in some form in practical Catholic preaching of the faith) is still far from having received its due measure of attention from theologians. It is, nevertheless, so clearly documented in the New Testament that it may well be termed a doctrine of faith. The traditional scholastic theological view, based on the Council of Trent (Denzinger 792), states only that the death of the Christian in the state of grace no longer has the mark of a punishment for sin, but, like concupiscence in the justified man, has the character of a mere consequence of sin *(poenalitas sed non poena)*, which is not abolished by God in order that it may serve for the testing and the purification of the just. We need not insist at this point that the concept of *poenalitas* as opposed to *poena*, of a consequence of sin as

67

opposed to its punishment, remains obscure so that it is difficult to see how, on the basis of this conceptual distinction, the death of the sinner and that of the just differ in reality. It would seem, according to this traditional opinion, that a merely external and legal consideration on God's part constitutes the entire difference. Nor do we wish to stress the fact that in this traditional opinion, death is viewed only from the angle of original sin, as still present or as deleted by baptism, while its relation to personal sin is not considered at all. One might ask, is the death of the baptized sinner only a "poenalitas"? Finally, we lay no stress on the fact that in this view, death appears only as an undesirable event, and not as a human action, though this latter characteristic intrinsically distinguishes the death of the sinner from that of the justified man. Even when all these difficulties are disregarded, the objection must still be made to the scholastic statement that it describes the death of the just man merely negatively. It offers no explanation of what constitutes this death positively as the death of a man in the state of grace, in spite of the fact that, merely by raising this issue, scholastic theology shows that it was to some degree aware of the need for establishing such a difference.

The New Testament, however, has more to say about the Christian's death. There is a "dying in the Lord" (Apoc 14:13; 1 Thess 4:16; 1 Cor 15:18), a death which is really no death at all, because, as Christ says, everyone who lives and believes in him shall never die (Jn 11:26). There is also a dying with Christ which is life-giving (2 Tim 2:11; Rom 6:8). We may content ourselves here with noting that, according to the New Testament, our assumption of Christ's death begins in principle with baptism and faith, while the process of dying with Christ, and obtaining new life thereby, secretly dominates life here on earth (Rom 6:6, 11 f.; 7:4–6; 8:2, 6–12, etc.).

These statements of the New Testament imply that physical death must be conceived as an axiological factor which dominates the whole of life, and also as an action. If we do not wish to dissolve our dying with Christ by faith and righteousness during this earthly Christ-formed life into an idealistic ethical conception, and thus lose contact with real death, we must recognize that, according to the New Testament, real death even when viewed as the final event of human life (qualified naturally by that life), is in the just a dying in Christ. That is to say that the death itself of a man in the state of grace is a saving event. Those who have died in faith are not "dead in Christ" only because they lived in Christ, but also because their dying itself was in Christ. We may even say that death is the culmination both of the reception and of the effecting of salvation, when we recall that death, as a human action, is precisely the event which gathers up the whole personal act of a human life into one fulfilment. We have only, too, to recall, as Eutychius (A.D. 582) said, that there occurs "pragmatically" in death what had occurred "mystically" at the sacramental heights of Christian life, in baptism and in the Eucharist, namely our assimilation to the death of the Lord. What occurs "sacramentally" in these moments of culmination, happens "really" in our death: the partaking in the death of our Lord.

We have so far only pointed out the fact; we have not said anything about how it takes place. Can anything be said about it? We shall attempt to. Let us consider again for a moment the death of Christ. The characteristic feature of his death is not that in some vague and general sense he died loving, self-sacrificing, obedient; in the ordinary sense, that is, in which any other event might just as well have been effected and endured in the right spirit and with the right attitude. What truly distinguished his death, is that death, as the manifestation of sin, became in him an expression of grace; the emptiness of man the advent of God's plenitude (which death certainly cannot of itself be). Death became life; visible condemnation became the visible advent of the Kingdom of God. All this is true not only in the sense that all these effects were produced by death and objectively caused by it through a moral causality. The full sense is that in Christ what of itself could only have been the experience of sin became, through his act which occurred in grace, something entirely different from what it appeared to be.

The real miracle of Christ's death resides precisely in this: death which in itself can only be experienced as the advent of emptiness, as the impasse of sin, as the darkness of eternal night (especially since the supernatural order is the real order in which there should be no death), and which "in itself" could be suffered, even by Christ himself, only as such a state of abandonment by God, now, through being embraced by the obedient "yes" of the Son, and while losing nothing of the horror of the divine abandonment that belongs to it, is transformed into something completely different, into the advent of God in the midst of that empty loneliness, and the manifestation of a complete, obedient surrender of the whole man to the holy God at the very moment when man seems lost and far removed from him. Through the fact of Christ's death, the justifying grace of God illustrates and confirms something which before it did not show but which was hidden from us; at the very moment in which sin reached its fullest measure, grace prevailed; it can even overcome sin. And through the death of Christ, when he surrendered himself to the innermost part of the world, this grace became ours. What he really accomplished in his death, and what his death really is, may be stated thus: his death, as an act of grace, helped to offer to God the "flesh of sin" – which death really is – transforming it into a flesh of grace; so that we now can, through his grace, belong to God and to Christ in death, despite the fact that death, in itself, means remoteness from God.

These considerations may make it possible to understand just what the Christian, in death, achieves through the grace of Christ (in the death which he effects throughout his life). He experiences his life falling into the emptiness and the powerlessness of death as remoteness from God, as the bitterness of guilt (his own and that of the human race), yet he believes in the mercy of God, hopes for life in God and loves this God so far removed from him. This faith, hope and charity are not, however, mere feelings accompanying the brutal reality of death, lasting only until death really occurs, persisting powerlessly beside the hard reality which is death. They are, rather, because transformed by grace, the true reality which transforms death but which, in order that faith should be preserved, transforms it in such a way that death is still experienced as the wages of sin. The trinity of faith, hope and charity makes death itself the highest act of believing, hoping, loving, the very death which seems to be absolute darkness, despair, coldness itself. These three fundamental powers of Christian life (together with grace, of which they are the

71

personal realization), entering death, receive the mode which characterizes them in Christian life in this aeon, that of submissive obedience: faith in darkness, hope against hope, love of God who appears only as Lord and as inexorable justice. In so far as these fundamental acts become constituents of death as an act of man, death itself is changed; the dreadful falling into the hands of the living God, which death must appear as a manifestation of sin, becomes in reality: "Into thy hands I commend my spirit."

Needless to say, these considerations by no means exhaust all there is to be said about the death of the Christian. For instance, as it corresponds to the positive meaning of Christ's descent into hell, it constitutes an arrival in the ground of the world, already glorified through Christ's death. We are also unable to discuss the Christian's attitude to death during this life, in so far as this attitude can, in some way, be distinguished from the effective presence of death through the whole of life. And we might have mentioned Christian vigilance, remembrance of the last things, waiting for the Lord, joy at his nearness, the groaning of the creation for redemption, even the glorification of the body as it perhaps begins even in this life, through a slow approach through the ascetic life to the ideal of Paradise, of freedom from concupiscence. These subjects must necessarily be passed over here because they would lead us too far afield into the areas of general or special eschatology and the general theory of Christian life.

3. The Sacramentally Visible Union between the Death of Christ and the Death of the Christian

The encounter between man and Christ, the pouring out of Christ's salvation, life and glory upon man, does not take place only in the sacraments, but whenever and wherever man, in grace, freely accepts God's grace. But this personal encounter between God and man in Christ can have an official, social, visible expression and embodiment in the Church, in the visible signs and rites established by Christ himself. These are the sacraments. Whenever man, with faith and love, opens himself to them, they cause in him, by virtue of the power of Christ and as acts of Christ, the effects of which they are the visible signs. That is to say, the grace of Christ becomes efficacious in the particular quality and direction that is signified by each sacramental rite. Their visible character does not embrace the whole of the Christian's life of grace; the latter is much more extensive and is intended to transform the whole life of man. Yet in the sacraments it is to be expected from the start that the most basic and decisive cases of the encounter of God and man in Christ will be given embodiment and made visible. The sacraments represent, in the life of the Christian, the visible form of the basic acts by which the redemption is appropriated.

The appropriation of Christ's death, which transforms the character of our own, is one of these basic acts; not, however, coming like a single point in time at the end of life, but rather as a process permeating its entire course. As a consequence, it might by expected that this appropriation of Christ's death should also have its visible sacramental form in the public life of the Church and this throughout our lives. And in fact it does. Even apart from the fact that by the nature of the case all the sacraments derive their strength and efficacy from Christ's redemptive death and thus all bring us into contact with his death (as the Fathers used to emphasize, all sacraments have their ultimate source in the pierced heart of the Redeemer), there are three sacraments in particular which, by their immediately perceptible form, by the meaning they express and according to the testimony of Scripture, make us partakers of Christ's death and, consequently, make our own death a participation in his: baptism, holy Eucharist and anointing of the sick.

Baptism plunges us into Christ's death, as St. Paul says (Rom 6:3). We are buried with him into his death (Rom 6:4), through baptism, which is the semblance of his death. We are conformed to the death of Christ (Phil 3:10). St. Paul conceives the effect of baptism as a sacramental assimilation to Christ's death (and in baptism by immersion, the burial is also symbolized); in baptism, man dies to sin, by "mortifying" in himself earthly, godless desires in order to live a new, holy life. In his view, consequently, there must be a real, intrinsic relationship between the mystical death in baptism and the actual death of the Christian, and not merely between baptism and the dying-to-sin during life. When St. Paul says: through baptism we are buried with him into death, in regard to Christ's death, death must be taken in the real sense; and the same will therefore be true in regard to our own death. In other words, St. Paul indicates a similarity between Christ and ourselves in our actual death, and this similarity is formed by baptism. Considered from this point of view, it is clear that

74

the dying-to-sin, which St. Paul emphasizes as the effect of our assimilation of Christ's death, is not a mere metaphorical use of the term "death"; he means by it, rather, our participation in Christ's death through our own real death, which is enacted perpetually throughout our lives and consummated in the actual death of the Christian. By life in grace, the Christian dies throughout life into his death as a dying with Christ. This real death, but one present throughout life, begins at baptism. Baptism is the sacramentally visible beginning of that death which is not the culmination of sin but of the appropriation of salvation which overcomes sin. Baptism is the beginning of Christian death, because it is the initiation of the life of grace, by virtue of which alone death can be Christian. We may even say that the life of grace *is* Christian death, if man's death is in fact the whole action of his life. It is to be noted, says Eutychius, that in holy baptism we die mystically (in modern terms, sacramentally) and then, whether in martyrdom or outside of it, in reality, objectively. Our mystical death is not different from the pragmatical one, even if it is only consummated in the pragmatical (*De Paschate* 5; PG, 86–2397). Through baptism we are crucified with Christ and the crucifixion of our Christian life is consummated in the act we call our death. Baptism as the beginning of Christian life is also the sacramental beginning of Christian dying. Anyone who in his life denies and brings to nought the power and the obligation of his baptism, resembles the robber hanging at the left hand of the Lord. Yet he is still near him. This was made visible when we were baptized.

It should be added that this companionship with the Lord in death, since death is present all through life, also includes companionship in his sufferings. Suffering, in fact, is nothing else than that *prolixitas mortis*, that long-drawn out death, as St. Gregory the Great calls life which is subject to suffering leading to death. That is why, since baptism, companionship with Christ in suffering is the realistic accomplishment of companionship in death during life and both therefore have their root in baptism.

The second sacrament which repeatedly and visibly reveals and deepens this companionship in suffering and death with our Lord, by grace throughout the whole course of the Christian life, is the sacred mystery of the Eucharist. This is the continuously renewed celebration of the death of the Lord, making that death present here and now in our lives. In the Eucharist, according to his command, we announce his death, which is our death and our life, again and again until he comes once more and it is no longer revealed in ritual sign but in the radiance of his visibly manifested glory, that in his death our death is swallowed up by the victory of life. What is done in this mystery is the sacramental enactment of Christ's death, and what we receive in this mystery is the grace which became ours, in his death. If the sacraments, in fact, perform the work which they symbolically express, then this sacrament, in which we announce the mystery of his death, must effect his death in us. In this sacrifice and sacrament, not only is the mystery of the Cross brought near to us in a spatio-temporal relation, but it actually produces its effect on our own lives, drawing us into itself, subjecting us to its own unfathomable laws and communicating its strength to us. Of necessity, therefore, anyone who takes part in this mystery in divine worship, announcing in it the death of the Lord, must also announce this death in his own life, by experiencing it in himself in the reality of his life. If it is true that Christ wishes in this sacrament day by day to be formed anew, he must do so by this sacrament in the form of the Crucified. For we must consider as the effect of this sacrament all that Scripture means by our communion in the passion and death of Christ: that we must suffer with him, in order to be glorified with him (Rom 8:17); that through participation in his passion we are conformed to his death (Phil 3:10); that he has to be glorified in our bodies in life and in death (Phil 1:20); that for Christ's sake we are constantly delivered into the power of death (2 Cor 4:10f.); that with him who was crucified in infirmity, we also are weak (2 Cor 13:4); that it is a grace, not only to believe in Christ, but also to suffer for him (Phil 1:29); that only if we have died with him shall we live with him (2 Tim 2:11). We share his death because we daily celebrate and receive the sacrament of his death.

In the visible sacramental signs of baptism and of the holy Eucharist we have clear reference to Christ's death and therefore to our own. The third sacrament, which we have still to consider briefly, anointing of the sick, manifests the relationship to Christ's death by the situation in which it is administered, the sickness of the body. We cannot here enter more fully into the theology of sickness. For Scripture and for faith, sickness is not merely a biological process, but, as a way to death and a danger of death, it is the visible manifestation of the power of sin and of the devil as well as of that weakness of man which, ethically and corporeally, is an expression of sin and of the danger of sin. Sickness is, therefore, eminently a situation of decision between salvation and damnation, and this just at a moment when man, precisely because he is sick, is in danger of not meeting this situation properly. It is, therefore, almost to be expected that in this situation of life, so important for man's salvation, the divine grace which we need to enable us to face it properly, should receive visible sacramental form. And in fact it does. The fifth chapter of the Epistle of James testifies that the priest of the community has authority to anoint the sick man with oil while praying for him. The effect of this sacramental action is called "salvation", that is, the Christian endurance of this decisive situation in life, either because bodily health is restored, or because he accepts his mortal illness in a Christian manner and endures death like a Christian. Since everyone must die sometime and is, therefore, to receive this sacrament in mortal sickness, it becomes the sacrament of the situation of the dying. In this case this sacrament assumes the character of a consecration to death, and becomes the visible manifestation of the fact that the Christian, confirmed by the anointment of the Lord, and in virtue of his grace, endures the last trial of his life, performs this last act, his own death, in companionship with the Lord.

We may, therefore, say that even if their relationship to the death of the Christian does not constitute the whole nature of these three sacraments, they have, nevertheless, a fundamental relation to it. Baptism, first of all, makes Christian death possible. The Eucharist continuously strengthens the life of the Christian in order that, through assimilation to Christ's death, his own life, in his daily actions and sufferings, may grow from within into that consummation which in death becomes definitive and is saved. The anointing of the sick is the consecration of the end of this life to the death of Christ. The beginning, the middle and the end of Christian life, as the appropriation of Christ's death, are signified and consecrated by these three sacraments.

We have spoken much of death, yet said very little. But who can say much of the mysteries of human existence, especially when they are taken into the very mysteries of God himself? And yet man must give thought to death, not only because his is a life moving towards death, but even more because death is a mystery of Christ the Lord. Since Christ died for the salvation of the world, and the life and glory of God, through the death of the Crucified, has been brought definitely into this world, there is nothing in all the world more important than this death. Compared with it, all other events are incidental and unimportant. Since we have received the vocation and the grace to die with him, the commonplace daily event called human death, towards which we all so reluctantly move, is raised into God's mysteries. In order to understand this mystery and to perform it worthily in the liturgy of our life, we only need contemplate the death of the Crucified, attend to and repeat the words which he uttered, so expressive of the lowest and highest aspects of death: "My God, my God, why hast thou forsaken me; Father, into thy hands I commend my Spirit." On each side of him, to right and left, with terrifying symbolism, two others hung in death. Two men, cursing death, because they could not understand it. But who can? One of them gazed at the death of Christ. What he saw was enough to make his own death comprehensible to him. Certainly a man who said to the dying Christ: "Lord, remember me, when thou shalt come into thy kingdom", had understood and correctly perceived the meaning of his own death. And the Son of Man, who shared our fate in death and redeemed it into life, said to that dying man: "Today thou shalt be with me in paradise." That is what he says to us, too. In order, however, that this message of a happy death should not take away the holy fear in which we have to work out that blessed death, he spoke no word to the other thief. The darkness and the deadly silence which hovered over this second death warn us that death can also be the beginning of eternal death. In this fear and trembling, however, we are to hear the good news of death, which is life, and of the coming of the Lord who is that life which knows no death, although it comes to us in death. This reality is still veiled by the sober reality of what we experience in dying. Nevertheless it is the truth that faith holds concerning death.

ON MARTYRDOM*

Martyrdom, as it is understood today, is death for the sake of Christian faith or Christian morals. Therefore, when speaking of death, martyrdom must also be discussed, if only as an epilogue. One must be careful, however, not to make this highest achievement, this most complete powerlessness, the pure grace of the Crucified, the dreadful fact that a man thrusts another into his irrevocable end through criminal arrogance and from a hatred of the faith (thinking he is doing a service to God), an object of empty talk or facile enthusiasm. It may be that in religious magazines the martyrs of the present day are praised, but in doctrinal studies they are mentioned only in a small corner of fundamental theology or apologetics. Yet this subject, taking into account what has been written on it in earlier ages, does provide matter for serious thought. The ancient authors certainly did not, for example, have occasion to discuss the case of martyrs whose personalities had been so crushed

* This is the substance of a lecture originally given independently of the foregoing Study on Death. If in this context, therefore, some material is repeated that was discussed previously, the author begs to be excused. This shorter exposition, however, may have its advantages.

in the bodily basis of the mind with a cunning unknown to past ages that they were physically unable to profess their faith, with the result that in the eyes of the world they did not have the fame of martyrdom at all, but stood there, apparently weaklings admitting their own dishonour. It is true Scripture says: "*nolite praemeditari*". But the way the Fathers praise martyrdom shows that they did not think it superfluous or foolish to examine seriously the extreme cases of Christian life.

Martyrdom is concerned with death. Although death does not belong to the original biblical concept of *martyrein*, of *martyria*, or *martyrion*, we can find already in the New Testament the beginnings of that history of the concept which, as early as the second century, led to the accepted meaning: a martyr is one who freely accepting his death in faith, is killed by powers inimical to Christ, and bears a noble testimony as a "witness" to faith in Jesus Christ. Since that period, the martyr, the "witness" as such, has been the witness through death.

But that does not answer but raises the precise question of the theological meaning of martyrdom. What is the fundamental connection between witness to Christ and death? Is it merely the result of the historical development of the concept, a more or less accidental and arbitrary conjunction of the two terms, "testimony" and "death", or are there some intrinsic links between them? By investigating this problem we may hope to gain some insight, however remote, into Christian martyrdom.

The connection and the common roots of the two realities of "witness" and "death", that hold them together, can be thought of in various ways. Of course, there are links between them which are rather obvious, even in the average view. One may be tempted simply to say that anyone who at the cost of his life and in spite of its sacrifice, remains faithful to his convictions, proves that he really takes his convictions seriously. His opinion must therefore be of a kind to make death-defying heroes. It may be added, that, as history testifies, Christianity has been rich in such a fidelity to the faith to the death and that in fact it has been so much richer than any other persuasion or ideology that this abundance of the spirit of martyrdom cannot be explained merely by the spiritual and moral powers native to the human heart, but that the Spirit from above, the Holy Spirit of grace and strength, alone can account for the countless band of those who have been killed for professing Christ, who consequently, are a proof that the foundations of Christianity are from above. Finally it may be added that since the "faithful witness" as such, Jesus Christ himself, went to his death, and since the disciple is not above his master, it should be obvious that the disciple has to follow in the bloody footsteps of his master and share the fate of the Word Incarnate unto death. All that is true and acceptable. And anyone who really understands what is meant by these traditional expressions, has probably understood everything, for then his faith, his love, his fidelity comprehend more than words actually explicitly express. However, in order to understand what is in those words, we must continue to ask questions as if we had understood nothing at all.

Martyrdom has to do with death. In order to understand martyrdom, death must be understood. And so the mystery of death enters into martyrdom, and makes martyrdom itself a mystery. One only dares approach the subject of death hesitantly. For the hidden incomprehensibility of death is also concealed from the average everyday mind, by the fact that death happens daily, and the dullard thinks that what happens every day must be understandable.

The mystery of death is only distorted if it is viewed on the same level as the end of the animals and is conceived as a biological event which, in a certain way, has only adventitiously anything to do with man as such, owing to the fact that his biological end concerns something which is rather more than a purely material living being. The real nature of death as a total and totally human event is completely missed if one takes cognizance only of the traditional definition: a separation of body and soul. For then death is seen only in one of its consequences, instead of in its essence, and we would have to force artificially and retrospectively into the expression, "separation of body and soul", those elements which constitute the special character of human death, namely, the personal finality of the end, the fully human and indissoluble unity of act and suffering in death, the hidden outcome of a life which is reaching its full accomplishment, the birth of that eternity, which is not simply added as the continuation of earthly time, but is rather the fruit of a final, free and absolute decision growing out of time itself, precisely inasmuch as it has been a human time.

From these and similar features of human death, which cannot be discussed here systematically in all their interconnections, let us select the one which has special bearing on the present topic: the voluntary character of death as such. Death is an act. Certainly it is the extreme case of something undergone, the event in which what is obscure and beyond control disposes of man, ineluctably taking him from himself, in the ultimate depth of his existence. Yet at the same time death is an act, and in fact the act of all acts, a free act. A man may be unconscious at the moment he is dying. Death may take him by surprise, if what we mean by death is the instant at the end, in which the death which we all die throughout our lives orientated towards this moment is manifested. But just because we die our death in this life, because we are permanently taking leave, permanently parting, looking towards the end, permanently disappointed, ceaselessly piercing through realities into their nothingness, continually narrowing the possibilities of free life through our actual decisions and actual life until we have exhausted life and driven it into the straits of death; because we are always experiencing what is unfathomable and are constantly reaching out beyond what can be stated, into what is incalculable and incomprehensible; and because it is only in this way that we exist in a truly human manner, we die throughout life, therefore, and what we call death is really the end of death, the death of death. Whether this death of death will be the second death or the killing of death and the victory of life, depends completely on us. Hence, because death is permanently present in the whole of human life, biologically and in the actual concrete experience of the individual person, death is also the act of human freedom.

It must however be observed that man has to die his death in freedom. He cannot avoid this death imposed upon him as the work of his freedom. How he dies his death and how he understands it, depends on the decision of his freedom. Here he does not carry something imposed on him, but what he chooses himself. That is to say that in the act of his dying human existence, man is in the necessity of freely adopting his attitude towards death. He is asked how he wills to do this. For when he opens the eyes of the mind at all, man inescapably sees the end, sees it all through life, perhaps dimly and not explicitly, perhaps deliberately avoids looking at it, "overlooks" it, but sees it all the same in doing so. And by freely accepting this human life orientated towards its end, man freely accepts the movement towards the end. But the question is, how does man understand this end towards which he freely moves, since he cannot do anything else than run the course of his life in freedom? Does he run protestingly, or lovingly and trustingly? Does he view his end as extinction, or as fulfilment? Men usually do not express their answer to this problem in abstract statements about death, but they live and tacitly carry out their free conviction through the actions of their life and the deeds of their daily existence, even when they do not know explicitly that by their life they are interpreting their death. We must therefore ask what, from the Christian point of view, is this right interpretation of the act of life which is death.

Here it must first be remembered that the liberty imposed has to be a free, a genuine liberty. Man cannot but be free once he has come to self-awareness. That is the freedom that is imposed. Man may hate this freedom; or he can want not to have it and pretend that it is not there. He can let himself drift; and in a cowardly and guilty manner he may regard himself merely as the product of his age and environment. But he ought to accept his freedom willingly and spontaneously, love it and have the courage for it. And he ought to respond in this way to freedom in its fullest sense, when it is concerned, not only with this or that, not only with the superficial aspect of life, but with life as a whole, down to its ultimate root; he ought, therefore, to have a liberty freely loved with regard to death. He should accept death freely, and should live towards death in real liberty. Anyone who fears death like an animal, with only its dumb life-instinct, and tries to hide from it, or directly attaches himself only to the vital fear of pain because he has not the courage to practise renunciation in calm training for the final renunciation, is in fact not yet the man he has to be. His attitude suppresses what primarily makes him different from animals, that is, knowledge of his own transcendence, which when really achieved, not merely thought about, by the mortal creature whom we call man, is only genuine in the form of a freely-admitted awareness of his own dedication to death. Wherever there is real liberty, there is love for death and courage for death.

But this real liberty in the courage to die has, secondly, to be a submissive liberty, that is, a liberty which says "yes" not only to death itself, but also to its meaning, to the meaning of human existence. Man should not hurry towards his death as towards the finite end of his existence, but as towards an infinite end. Not towards a death which is the consummation of vacuity, a final emptying of life into meaninglessness, but towards a death which is the valid fulfilment of his existence. This, however, can be done only in faith. The eternally valid fulfilment in death cannot be grasped by mortal man, who is to posit death freely, as something that is simply there; for death as the pitch of evanescence, of all that is transitory, which is all that is perceptible in it, does not fulfil existence but seems finally to annihilate it.

Death is a fall, and only by faith can this fall be interpreted as a falling into the hands of the living God, who is called

Father. Since this affirmative interpretation of man's mortal life in a disposal over the whole of life, can only take place, as we as Christians know, by the grace of Christ, because in the present order of sinful darkness the whole of life can be mastered in a morally right way only by the grace of God, then the act performed in virtue of the grace of Christ, whereby man positively accepts the comprehensive sense of his human existence in face of the sinister appearance of meaningless death, can and must necessarily be called an act of faith: the surrender of the whole man in the incalculability and impenetrability of human existence to the incomprehensible God. Whenever a man dies in this way, freely, believing and trusting, detached from all that is particular and concrete in the frank confidence that in this way he will obtain everything, at the point where he is apparently experiencing a collapse into emptiness, into the fathomless abyss, he is doing something that cannot be done except by the grace of Christ which celebrates its victory thereby. There a man is not dying the death of Adam, the death of the sinner in his love of what is nothing provided it is at his own disposal. Whether he knows it or not, a man is dying the death of Christ, for only Christ's death gained this grace for us and only his death freed our death into the life of God himself.

These statements are made with a clear realization of the theological difficulties they involve. It could be argued for instance, that, according to theologians, in addition to supernatural and meritorious acts, there are also naturally moral acts, *actus honesti,* and that such acts are possible, not only in the abstract (for the distinction between nature and nature's supernatural elevation and divinization by grace is unquestionably a part of Catholic theology which has been repeatedly defended by the *magisterium*), but also in the realm of concrete fact. This could occur wherever man acts freely, but because of culpable or inculpable lack of faith, which is the beginning of supernatural saving action, is incapable of a supernatural moral act and yet cannot simply be sinning in each of his free acts, presuming, of course, that this lack of faith is not culpable and that his act has not otherwise an evil motive. From this it follows (so the argument continues) that a person could die, accepting death as God's will in a morally right surrender, that is, that he could die a non-sinful death, which still would not be an act of faith proper, since *(ex supposito)* the *fides ex auditu* has not reached him, and, therefore, he is only capable of acts of natural morality and not of an act of that faith which derives essentially from acceptance of an historical message of the living God.

To answer this difficulty, it would be sufficient to mention that such cases represent border-line or marginal problems and thus do not exclude the fact that, in the normal instance (and most theologians will admit that normal instances are far from being restricted to the officially Christian world), men confronted by faith or unbelief either die the death of faith or the death of real infidelity, that is, the Christian or the un-Christian death; in neither case would they die a death which would be neutral in regard to salvation. We can, however, go even further. Even if we must distinguish nature from its supernatural elevation by grace, nevertheless even in modern theology it is possible to contest whether in fact there are any morally significant but supernaturally neutral acts. Though the problem cannot of course be discussed fully here, it cannot be

89

totally ignored. The following observations seem, then, in order.

The question is to decide whether the highest act of spiritual and moral man, his total disposal of himself in death, can really be indifferent in relation to salvation. Following Ripalda, different ways might be tried of showing that the possibility of merely natural, good moral acts is never actually realized in the really existing economy of salvation. In the first place it could be asked how a naturally good moral act can coexist with God's universal salvific will in regard to all men, even after original sin. Cases of such naturally good acts would after all have to be sought only and precisely where a man without personal guilt – on this supposition, such a condition must be made – is incapable of that faith which is the beginning and prerequisite of all other supernatural moral acts. But if some man without any personal guilt is incapable of a supernaturally meritorious act, it is not really possible to see how God can really have the will to save this man. One cannot reply that this man is not in such a position of inability throughout his life, and that God, by his supernatural providence in regard to salvation, will offer him some concrete possibility of supernatural acts, even a man who (for the greater part of his life) through no fault of his own has been far removed from supernatural faith. In definite terms, then, how is this possibility that is offered at some point to this man to be envisaged? Of what kind is it to be if its realization is to sound convincing, and not to be of a kind that is always present and yet for a time was not present? Let us take as an example a pagan, who in his pagan environment can hardly be considered likely to have the opportunity to respond to a message of revelation coming to him in history. God's universal salvific will cannot meaningfully be bound by conditions which remain unrealized because of divine providence alone, and yet represent, at the same time, a serious will to save all. The fate of children dying without baptism cannot apply here. Instead of helping to solve the problem, it would only aggravate it. Moreover the salvation of an adult is endangered in a quite different way from that of a child. If it is pointed out that, in the case of unbaptized infants, God's salvific will is simply not the same as for adults, we can say that the converse also holds. Finally, it is by no means clearly determined whether these children are really excluded from supernatural salvation.

Furthermore it must also be considered that the free possibility of salvation through grace does not include in its concept (although this is readily assumed) that salvation is only for the few. Grace is no less grace simply because it is seriously offered to all in such a manner that it can be lost only through personal guilt. The opinion, which we question here (we do not wish to say more than that it is questionable) suggests, after all, that God establishes an order of supernatural salvation; that he imposes it as a strict duty upon all men; that, however, he constructs this order in such a manner and links its realization to such conditions that actual concrete, and therefore supernatural, moral life in this order is impossible for many men and indeed for very many men, without any guilt on their part. St. Augustine was more honest and more logical in this matter, in assuming that, since original sin, God has only a more particular salvific will. Supposing, however, it is admitted that at least among men who reach the use of reason there are very few who, without any personal guilt, do not attain eternal happiness, because everyone, including all the men who through thousands of years have lived outside the official history of salvation in the Old and the New Testaments, at some time is confronted with the concrete opportunity of attaining supernatural salvation, and unless an attempt is made to evade this conclusion by saying that, in the case of many men, this chance in concrete and immediate form does not have to be offered because they make themselves unworthy of it in advance through grave transgression of the moral law (as though God does not have an effective salvific will in regard to sinners); then that offer of a concrete opportunity for men to secure supernatural salvation through their own acts has to be conceived (at least, the attempt has to be made to conceive it, if theology is not to be made unbelievable) in such a way that it is realized without recourse to miracles, which, after all we know by experience, do not happen every day.

The opinion we contest confuses in our opinion the conditions of salvation with the conditions of its tangible historical form and visibility. Catholic theology holds firmly that the conditions for conferring a sacrament and the conditions for receiving the grace which, in the normal way of salvation, is received through this sacrament are not identical. This insight should be kept more clearly in view and applied more consistently. The sacraments and the message of faith, in its tangible historical form (which when the matter is considered, belong to the same order) are the normal, divinely ordained way of salvation. They are willed by God, because he willed not only salvation but also the historical incarnation of salvation. This means that he wills not only grace but also sacrament, not only a community of saints in invisible grace but also a socially organized Church and so on. And he obliges us to conform to this order for our actions, wherever we are capable of so doing. But God did not bind himself and his grace to the order he prescribed for us, for he cannot make it impossible for himself to attain what he himself wills. The final salvation of man can only be willed or not willed (so far as it concerns simply God's own activity and not the freedom of the other partner). This will is, like salvation itself, ultimately *in indivisibili*. But the historical realization of this salvation in this manifold, multi-dimensional, mutable world, is by the nature of the case divisible, permits realization part by part. In this respect God may will in very different degrees: in fact precisely these different grades or degrees in the world. Thus he can permit one person to receive baptism and another not to, and so on. But it is rash and basically false to conclude from this that exactly the same relation holds good between God's grace and the final salvation of man. It should first be proved that always and in each case there is an absolutely fixed and direct relation between the order of the historical incarnation of salvation and salvation itself. This is, however, fundamentally not a Catholic opinion and is in fact already superseded in principle in the Church, even though the consequences of this have not yet been developed with sufficient clarity. And all this does not mean that salvation is simply bestowed even on a man who has attained the use of his freedom, in a way that by-passes his freedom and therefore without his knowledge.

If therefore the question is asked, in what concrete way can we envisage the permanent situation of man whereby in whatever historical situation and at whatever distance from historical Christianity of an explicit kind grasped by the man himself, he can posit a supernatural act and so attain salvation, various answers are conceivable, even if in view of the above considerations one particular positive answer is thought to be correct. We could say, for example, that every man is of course not always and in all historical situations of humanity capable of making an explicit decision by faith in regard to the preaching of faith which comes to him as an historical event from the revelation given in history. A so-called *fides late dicta* (faith in some broader sense), which is, formally, nothing else than a metaphysical knowledge of God gathered from the consideration of nature, is not sufficient either. But whenever man arrives at a free decision about himself, he is always capable of a *fides virtualis,* that is, capable of an interior attitude towards God which is morally of the same kind as faith proper, and which can thus become, when elevated by an interior grace, a saving act and (if the grace is not freely rejected), exist as such. The readiness to believe, the "faithful" openness to the silent namelessness of God and his call coming as yet inarticulately ("Speak, Lord, for thy servant heareth"), all that, if elevated by grace (and why should it not be so transformed supernaturally and be made by God a dynamic force leading into eternal life?), becomes a supernatural moral act, virtually equivalent to actual faith in the gospel sent by God.

At the same time, it should be remembered that the supernatural elevation of an act, according to the correct (even if disputed) theological opinion, also involves an essential change of the act in *consciousness* (even though this need not mean that new contents of consciousness are conceptually present).

If that is the case, however, it is even easier to understand why such an act is virtually equivalent to a proper, explicit and formal act of faith, and also why such an act, if at the same time it is love, has power to justify.

Briefly, what was to be pointed out here was that (reviving Ripalda's opinion) it is far from certain that there are any purely natural moral acts even *in concreto*. There are many reasons against them, because by assuming that purely natural moral acts actually occur, the concrete order, instead of consisting of a situation of sin and supernatural salvation, is split into a threefold order of reality (and not only of possibility), and where moral decision is made, a neutral zone intrudes between salvation and perdition. If we follow Straub, it is possible, in a way that has never been rejected by the Church, to conceive the situation of every man in such a way that whenever he is obliged to make a moral decision, he is always deciding between his supernatural salvation or perdition, and consequently in the concrete is making his decision *within* the supernatural order as such. This suggestion had to be introduced here because we must investigate whether the highest moral act, whereby man freely consummates his whole existence (in other words, his free death), can be performed without making use of the highest opportunity offered to man by God, that is, without responding affirmatively to the God of *supernatural* life. If we are reluctant to admit the possibility of innocently missing the final peak of life which, after all, in itself is an obligation binding on every man, then we have to reject the idea that death can be a moral act of the merely natural order without relation to salvation or perdition. But in that case, willingly or unwillingly, whether or not this problem has been resolved by theology, whether or not it clashes with old accepted ideas, we have to pose and answer the question of whether there are any merely natural moral acts or not. If we say no (and if it is possible to do so without coming into conflict with the teaching authority of the Church), then the road is open to conceiving death as the comprehensive act of faith or unbelief, without having to reckon with the real possibility that it could be something less than the decision between the two extreme possibilities of human existence.

We may say, then, that Christian death is the freely exercised liberty of faith, which in reality and truth disposes of the whole of life, by accepting the incalculability of this mortal existence as a meaningful and loving disposition of God.

This act of free and believing liberty which takes place, which must and can take place in death, is, however, veiled. Death can of course also be an act of enforced liberty, a death of dumb despair, a letting oneself fall into dark emptiness instead of into the hands of the incomprehensible but beloved God. This veiled character of a death which comprises the whole quality of a completed life, does not derive simply from the fact that everything done freely by man, both in his own eyes and, even more, in the eyes of the world and in the eyes of empirical history, remains ambiguous and impossible to judge. This ambiguity of all freedom in fact reaches its supreme and unique culmination in death. Any other act in this world leaves behind a part of its reality which, to the doer and his fellow-men, offers the possibility of at least a partial judgment in regard to the whole of the action. In death, however, deed and doer disappear from the range of observation of doer and spectators into the mystery of God's sole judgment. Moving from these apparent digressions directly to the subject in hand, we may inquire whether this veiled death can somehow be revealed to us even here, as truly a death of genuine liberty and of real faith? Is there a death which can expose its dark, veiled essence to us and so enable us to know how a particular man really died? Is there a death in which the appearances disclose the reality? If there is such a revealing and patently evident Christian death, then it would constitute Christian witness as such, because the act integrating all that is Christian and perfecting a life, would also manifest what it is. Such a death would be a "fine death" expressing that ultimate beauty which is born of the perfect harmony between interior reality and external appearance. Such death would be the beautiful testimony (μαρτυρεῖν τὴν καλὴν ὁμολογίαν: 1 Tim 6:13) absolutely as such. Such a death would have to be loved and desired in spite of all anguish and horror, if man does in fact seek true reality as well as its true appearance, because here true reality and its true appearance are achieved and found most fully. Such an unveiling of the Christian essence of death exists in the martyrdom of the believer.

In order to disclose death as the act of genuine liberty (as the first property we have attributed to a truly Christian death), it must be a death which could have been avoided in the particular case. It must, then, be a death caused by external violence and which could have been avoided in its causes by the exercise of freedom of the threatened victim. If someone through his free act can avoid death, then one thing is manifestly accomplished which must be present in each Christian death, though it is mostly veiled and difficult to judge, that is, its free acceptance. Then is revealed the presence of that love of death which a Christian must have, and which he may not, however, carry into effect by suicide. Here is fulfilled what Jesus said of his own death: "I have the power to lay down my life." This is particularly true at that moment when we seem most fully under the domination of external forces: nobody takes my life, I myself lay it down. And this is exactly what does happen in the martyr's death; it is a free death. All the violence which causes it is only the secret device of God who provides the opportunity for this highest act of liberty, a liberty which man may not arrogate to himself or have granted to him by any other means; for although he possesses (even if not to so great a degree) liberty over his life (whereby he can exercise his choice and by so doing choose his death), he still possesses it only, as it were, anonymously and simply as extended over his whole life. In a violent death which could have been avoided and which is, nevertheless, accepted in freedom, the freedom of a whole life is gathered into the one burning moment of death. Then the death of life (in its totality and freedom) enters into the death of death, in an act of complete freedom affecting the totality of life and so life's eternal finality. The death of martyrdom is a death of genuine liberty. By it is disclosed what is elsewhere hidden under the veil covering death's essence. By it the enigma and veil of death (is it a death of enforced freedom or real liberty?) receives a definite answer.

When and how is a death a death whereby faith is revealed? This is our second question. One might think, at first glance, that it is easy to answer, for where is it more fully revealed that the death which is entered upon is an act of free faith in the victory of Christ's death, than in the death of the man who dies for his faith in the crucified and risen Lord, that is, in martyrdom? It might therefore seem obvious that martyrdom includes that quality which is essential to any right death, namely, that it must be a death of faith, and not a death of mute or open despair. But the solution is not so simple. For it might be asked whether the death of a martyr is in fact exempt from the general law that every moral decision remains ultimately enigmatic, for oneself and certainly for others. Was the good really done? And even if it were the right thing, something objectively good, such as the fulfilment of a divine precept or of the gospel counsels, can we be certain that it was motivated from within by faith and love, and that it proceeded from the grace of God, that is, from motives all beyond the observation of self and of others, so that no one is justified except by God's sole judgment? Even in the case of the martyr's death, does not the radical problem still remain unanswered whether an act which is good in itself is necessarily good in execution, and whether anything that we see happening will remain valid when it is weighed upon God's scale?

There is, after all, the death of the fanatic, of the hero, of the sectarian and of many others who die courageously and voluntarily. Although we pay the tribute of our respect to the monstrous and inexpressible greatness which may be found in those deaths, yet as Christians we do not attribute to them the same objective dignity and meaning which we recognize in martyrdom. At the same time, we do not need to deny in the individual case that the value of such a death, revealed only before God, may extend even to God and his eternal life. But in view of all this, the problem of the unique and manifest quality of Christian martyrdom obviously cannot be solved too easily. Yet on this solution depends our understanding of how it is possible to attribute to martyrdom the intrinsic character of testimony. In other words, why is death in faith a death bearing witness, a martyrdom, in the eminent sense?

To see the problem in its proper perspective we must study its background. The Church is holy Church. She is holy even in her historical, empirical reality; she is holy not only in her hidden essence, but she also "appears" as holy. The historical manifestation of the holiness of the Church does not consist only in an "objective" sanctity, that is, in the truth and holiness of her doctrine, or in the holiness of the divine grace she communicates to men, but in her "subjective" sanctity as well. The Church of poor sinners appears again and again as what she is, through the greater power of God's grace definitively, triumphantly and eschatologically established in the world, the community of those in whom grace and its victory has already begun "to be here", for whom the transformation of the old aeon into the glory of the new is not asserted only by a mere paradox of belief in contradiction to all experience, but is rather already perceptible, visibly emerging. This perceptible and historically ascertainable sanctity is not simply one of the essential characteristics of the Church, but is also a testimony, a motive of faith for the Church. This empirical appearance of the Church's holiness is diffused as it were throughout her history, in her works and in her deeds, which we call "holy" in the most profound sense.

This empirical reality, which is the manifestation of the truly victorious divine grace itself and not only some necessarily ambiguous semblance of it, if it appears at all, must be manifested in a precise and certain manner where the highest expression of faith and love is found, that is, in martyrdom, where death bears witness to faith. ·

If the Church is indeed to be subjectively holy and if this holiness is really to appear as a work of God's grace, then, if anywhere, it must be seen in martyrdom. Divine power, in order to sanctify the Church and to show her to be holy, must here overcome any cleavage between man's existence in the eyes of God and his existence in the eyes of the world, between supra-historical truth and historical appearance, between interior spirit and empirical fact. What appears here, death with Christ for God, must really be present. Here something must be done, not only by man who in himself is always ambiguous, but by the power of God victorious in human weakness. True consent to God and affirmation of his Word must ring out from the innermost centre of man, where nothing remains but the eternal man and his God, penetrating into earthly space and time, an affirmation unalloyed, God's truth. Outwardly man dies in faith, and death really occurs in loving faith in the most authentic truth and reality, guaranteed by that victorious eschatological grace which constitutes the Church as "sacrament" of God's holiness and grace. A martyr's death is not only death through man's freedom, but also the revelation of death in faith. Martyrdom is, therefore, Christian death as such. It is not only what Christian death in general should be, but it appears as such as well. Martyrdom discloses the essence of Christian death,

death in freedom and faith, which otherwise is hidden under the ambiguity of all human events.

Martyrdom thus belongs to the essence of the Church. It is to be expected, then, that there will always be martyrs in the Church, for she has not only to live as a witness to the crucified Christ, but she also has' to demonstrate visibly this living testimony. She cannot celebrate and make present the death of Christ only in the sacramental mystery of the Mass. She herself must live it in all truth. And she does live it in all those who carry the cross of Christ in the darkness of this world and who possess the secret stigmata of Christ hidden under the everyday appearance of their humanity. But if the Church is not only internally the reality of grace, but also its visible "sacrament", the holy sign of the intrinsic reality, in this world, then the crucified character of the Church too must be repeatedly manifested until the end. The most conspicuous and emphatic way for this public manifestation until the end is martyrdom.

From this we can understand why tradition from earliest times attributed to martyrdom the same power of justification as to baptism. Martyrdom possesses this power not merely because as an act of believing love it justifies even before reception of the sacrament like any other act of charity. The justifying power of martyrdom is, as it were, of a sacramental kind, for it is the manifestation of a grace-given reality; it is the empirical expression of a divine act of grace in man. Martyrdom cannot be called a sacrament in the common sense of the word because it does not belong to the daily and normal order of the holy signs instituted by Christ; such a death is always something extraordinary. Another reason is that, in martyrdom, what had previously been signified and made present through the sacramental sign of baptism is here simply fulfilled, namely dying and being baptized into the death of Christ. But even if we cannot call martyrdom a sacrament in the usual sense of the word, we refuse it this title, not because it is something less than a sacrament, but because it is something more. In the case of the ordinary sacraments, in spite of their objective character as *opus operatum,* which God in his power, offering his grace objectively, produces, a divergence between the ritual performance and the subjective reception is possible, so that, in fact, there may not be effected what is demonstrated by the objective sign. A man may not actually receive the grace which he appears to receive. In the appearance of martyrdom, however, such a mere semblance is *a priori* excluded. Wherever martyrdom is celebrated in blood, God's grace is truly victorious in the depth of reality. We might almost say that martyrdom is the only "supra-sacrament" which does not admit of an obstacle in the receiver, and in which the valid sacrament is always fruitful to eternal life. If it is asked where there is a point in human life where appearance is absolutely true and truth absolutely made manifest, a point where all is focussed, action and suffering, the commonplace and the incomprehensible, death and life, freedom and violence, the most human and the most divine, the dark sinfulness of this world and the grace of God embracing it in mercy, rite and reality, there is only one answer: in martyrdom and nowhere else. What appears here is and must be possible also in us if we are to be those who are redeemed, sanctified, who have died with Christ and have risen with him into newness of life. However, what appears here is what we should be, what we hope we are, but what, without martyrdom, we cannot be certain of. And what is here apparently, is here also in fact. Here the sign infallibly produces what it signifies and overcomes that ambiguity and uncertainty which attaches even to the sacraments since they can be received unworthily. This sacrament of blood can only be received worthily, or it cannot be received at all.

In martyrdom, therefore, we have an indissoluble unity of testimony and what is testified, guaranteed by God's gracious dispensation. Here there is accomplished with absolute validity and perfection what is testified: authentic Christian life as victorious grace of God. The testimony makes present what is testified and what is testified creates for itself its own authentic attestation. Word and thing here become one and they are perceived in their indissoluble unity. Of course, on man's part there could be mute acquiescence or empty words. From the human point of view, as may occur in the case of other voluntary deaths, it is possible to have just an empty show, or the bare shadow of reality. But God's act in his victorious grace prevents such discrepancy, bears witness to man fulfilled, in order to testify to itself by its own irrevocable realization in the flesh.

Church and martyrdom bear witness to one another. In the verbal testimony of the Church to eschatologically victorious grace, we obtain the innermost interpretation of martyrdom. It is really what it seems to be, a really comprehensive expression of world-conquering faith, the fulfilment of man. Martyrdom testifies on behalf of the Church. The fact that in her there have been so many such deaths throughout her history; that there is this death of radical sacrifice without fanaticism, pure greatness without histrionics, under the hatred of enemies with satanic power, and that this death is loved by those who do not hate the world, of itself testifies to the supernatural origin of the Church for those who, by the grace of God, are capable of seeing, even prior to the deeper inter-pretation of martyrdom which it only receives through the testimony of the Church. The Church, the lonely act of unique individual responsibility, speech and silent dying, hatred of the world and the love of God, death and life – they are all one here. If in the liturgy of the Mass the death of the Lord, and our own death in him, is mystically celebrated and if, in this celebration, the Church attains the perfect ritual fulfil-ment of her nature, the same thing happens in death by Christian martyrdom in which the Lord continues until the end of time to suffer and to triumph "pragmatically", as Eutychius said 1500 years ago.

Before concluding these reflections, one question should be more thoroughly considered, which previously was dealt with rather too briefly, until the matter could be viewed as a whole. We have noted that it is the very nature of the Church, as the triumphant visible manifestation of God's eschatological grace in the world and in history, which guarantees that in martyrdom there cannot exist any cleavage between the ob-jective goodness of the deed and the subjective goodness of the doer, between the appearance and the thing itself, be-tween the "sacrament" and the "grace of the sacrament". We said that martyrdom is the precise point where the objective and the subjective sanctity of the Church converge. Now in the first place that is a truth of faith, not an empirical one, which implies that an external observer cannot simply ascertain this character of martyrdom as an unambiguous, no longer dialectical, saving event. He knows that it is so, only if and because he believes in the eschatological, holy Church, and in the victory of the grace of God as an event which is already dawning. We also said that the martyr's death is a testimony which provides a reason and motive for faith in the Church, and is not only an object or part of already existent faith in the Church. But, then, must not martyrdom even empirically bear its character as God's testimony upon it, precisely if it is to be convincing testimony and a motive of faith? Until now on this problem we have simply pointed out briefly that by the great number of martyrs in the Church, by their patience, their lack of fanaticism, by the world's hatred which inflicts martyrdom and displays an evil and satanic character, and by other similar factors, which need not be further developed, martyrdom proves itself to be a miracle of divine grace. This means that anyone who considers martyrdom in the Church, as it is, will be able to distinguish it clearly from any other type of voluntary death for an ideal, for an ideology etc.; he will be able to realize that Christian martyrdom (even prior to the interpretation given it by faith) is not merely one of the many cases in the world and in history of "defending one's convictions unto death". If we were to elaborate these differences (which is not possible here), it could be pointed out that an essential of Christian martyrdom is the voluntary and believing acceptance of death itself and not merely the acceptance of the consequence of a struggle, as in the case of a brave soldier who seeks victory, not death. And so the significance of martyrdom for fundamental theology and for apologetics would be clearer. At the same time, we should always remember that even the most objective testimonies and arguments for the faith, which precede it as the basis of its moral and rational justification, and which in themselves are rationally knowable, are in fact recognized as grounds of faith only by those who are helped by the grace of God to see that they are and are intended as grounds of credibility, of free decision, and not merely the basis of knowledge and learning of a kind that involves neither moral decision nor an act of trusting freedom.

It may be questioned, however, whether this thesis of current fundamental theology exhausts what should be said about martyrdom either regarding its function as a foundation of the faith or its nature as testimony. We may get closer to the problem by asking: how do we make this identification between the objective excellence of the death and the subjective goodness of the manner of its acceptance? What assurance have we that this identity in no case breaks down? Naturally, we can and must answer, that it is through the grace of God, which decrees that this manifestation of death, whereby grace itself becomes forever triumphant, should never be a mere empty semblance. One might, however, go on to inquire how grace achieves this identification between thing signified and its sign. Is it possible to say more about it? Is there something in the nature of death which enables it to be such an indubitable manifestation?

It is not permissible to say that every voluntary death, no matter how and for what it is undergone, is necessarily a morally good one. Opposed to this is the Christian doctrine which condemns suicide as objectively wrong. But perhaps death voluntarily accepted, inflicted by others without provocation on the victim's part is always, *eo ipso,* a just death? That, too, cannot always be affirmed. The death of a heretic or of a fanatic will never be accepted simply and immediately by Christian feeling as of equal rank with martyrdom for the Christian faith. It cannot be admitted that the objective matter, in regard to which a moral attitude is realized, may *a priori* be so absolutely neutral as regards the successful achievement of this right attitude, that two actions which on the level of objective reality are contradictory not only may in fact be performed with the same moral attitude (for this certainly may occur), but also that the two actions equally and of themselves necessarily and inevitably involve the same moral attitude. If any freely accepted death were, *eo ipso,* a morally good death, then precisely as a death, that is, as the sum-total of the accomplishment of human life, it would always and in every case constitute the summit of life's moral achievement. But then the reason of the voluntary acceptance of death would lose all moral significance, not only in fact and in many cases, but in principle and in all cases. That assumption would have grave consequences for the whole of morality. The "attitude of mind" would become independent of any requirement of content. Consequently, it is not possible to canonize any voluntary death *a priori* and without further ado.

But this again is only one aspect of the question. Voluntary death cannot be regarded as a morally neutral matter, which derives its significance solely externally from a particular motive divorced from the death as such. Man of course has a unique feeling of reverence for any voluntary death which could have been avoided. Why is this reverence justified despite the reserves that have had to be expressed? In the first place, whenever someone dies freely, the whole of his life is present. This presence of the whole life, of the whole spirit and of freedom, commands our awe, if ever anything in man can be said to deserve our awe. Furthermore, death which is refused, the ineluctable death of the unfaithful and despairing, is not even in its formal constitution the same as the freely accepted death in faith. Good and bad freedom are not simply the same activation of the same liberty only in different directions and towards different objects. Just as freedom, as an intentional power, is specified by its object, so it is itself really specified by this object, that is, it is different in itself according to the different objects towards which it is directed. And it can be described through this difference, which is intrinsic to it, no matter whether such description of the influence of the object intended (the motive) on the subjective side of the act is totally or only partially successful. If it is possible to describe the difference in the subjective act, according to whether it is morally good or bad from this subjective angle, then, in certain circumstances, this quality will reveal whether its intentional object is really good or evil. That in itself is not particularly strange. There must be in some way a divinely ordained preestablished harmony between the subjective uprightness of the act and its intentional content; the materially good act cannot in the last resort be subjectively a perverse one, and vice versa. On this basic supposition rests, for instance, the whole doctrine of the Discernment of Spirits in St. Ignatius Loyola.* The

---

* Cf. K. Rahner, "Die ignatianische Logik der existentiellen Erkenntnis. Über einige theologische Probleme in den Wahlregeln der Exerzitien des hl. Ignatius von Loyola" in F. Wulf, *Ignatius von Loyola. Seine geistliche Gestalt und sein Vermächtnis* (Würzburg 1956), 345—405.

intentional difference in the acts involves an entitative difference (to speak even more scholastically), and an act which is false in the intentional order cannot conform entitatively with the being and well-being of the entitative faculty and with the being of the whole subject as well as an intentionally good act can. This might be possible in the case of insignificant acts, particularly if they are of the sensual order rather than the spiritual; for example, one may get a headache when doing a sum just as readily from a correct as from an incorrect answer. However, if it is a question of fundamental acts and the total realization of man's powers, this difference must be recognizable. Liberty for good is the stronger liberty; it is a freedom in which man is involved in his totality, a liberated freedom which blossoms and flows. Evil liberty fails, wills too little, shrinks from pure and unconditional giving; it is anxious, it counts and calculates; it is full of suspicion and is afraid of purifying suffering. Evil freedom, in comparison with true freedom, always displays outward symptoms of inferior objective and personal power. This applies, above all, to the fullness of freedom which is to be realized in death, and especially to voluntary death. Therefore death has an inner dynamic tendency .towards the highest and strongest act of man, of his strongest freedom. Consequently death, wherever it is accomplished purely according to its nature, will be a good death, even though we must not exclude the possibility of an evil death. To deny this statement would be to imply that good and bad deeds are ontologically and personally of the same value. Such a doctrine is absolutely contradictory to a scholastic ethics founded on being. A bad death is necessarily also a defective death, one that is not complete, a disintegrating fall, because man is afraid of the infinite fall into the liberty of God. Wherever, then, we encounter a death which has not been evaded, which has been accepted as such, which has not only just "happened" (even though clearly envisaged), and which has been in itself the object of free decision, then this must be a good death. In particular cases this cannot, perhaps, be completely determined; perhaps in particular cases some doubt will remain as to whether it has been a good death or a bad one. As noted, good and bad deaths are differentiated from each other, not only by their respective motivations (when a voluntary death is in question), but also by the manner in which the death is accomplished. In itself, however, this essential qualitative difference is discernible. When a man dies patiently and humbly, when death itself is seen and accepted, when it not merely "happens" in the course of striving for something else and when perhaps death is not really envisaged through blind eagerness for something (flight from shame, something obstinately sought etc.), when death is loved for its own sake, and explicitly, it cannot but be a good death. Whenever it is faced in a spirit of pure and free submission to the absolute decree, it is a good death. And this quality can be sufficiently verified by observation.

It may be that the above exposition does not adequately describe the subjective aspect of that death which can only be good. But this does not alter the fact that this subjective quality of death which manifests its goodness (its peace, patience, calm and deliberate gravity, its detachment) is fundamentally observable; it does not alter the fact that these conditions do become known even when the impression which they engender can only be very imperfectly analysed.

One more point should be added: in Christian martyrdom, it is death itself that is the theme. Death is not something which is merely accepted as a risk in stubborn pursuit of some definite aim, with obstinate, self-willed consistency, but it is something that is loved in itself, a sharing in our Lord's death, the blessed gate of eternal life. Certainly the opponent has no right to kill, but the Christian martyr does not undergo death as something to which he has provoked another man, for in that case he might, with Kierkegaard, wonder whether he was justified in doing so "for the sake of a little truth". Death, for him, is something to which he is disposed by virtue of his whole existence.

It might be asked whether such a death does occur, as an historical tangible reality, in the actual spiritual history of humanity, except in Christianity. This question must probably be answered in the negative. But this should cause surprise, for death is obviously something which man should be able to deal with, on which man with his introspective self-knowledge (unlike the mere animals) should be able to focus attention. In fact, however, only Christianity succeeds in doing so. This arises from the perhaps merely factual but in fact unique correspondence which exists between what a Christian should do and what he believes. First, he should, as a human being, die a free death. Apart from the Christian, nobody does do this (naturally, the anonymous Christians, those who are Christian in spirit, though not in name, should be included here, provided they do not die for anything opposed to Christianity). Second, he believes, as a Christian, in the death of Christ as the only redemption. He therefore believes precisely in what basically constitutes the sum of his own existence. The manner in which a man dies shows death to be admitted and accepted in the very depths of his spiritual person, where not only abstract and theoretical ideals conceptually formulated are at stake, but where a man is really and truly himself. That is where death is accepted, and by a man whose theoretical views – those precisely for which he dies – justify in theory what he does in reality.

It might be said, perhaps, that this unity between theory and actual practice in the acceptance of death, the one being the motive for the other, is not specifically Christian, because such a death could also be prescribed and fulfilled on the basis of natural ethics. But looking, on the one hand, at world history as a whole, it becomes evident that this unity can be demonstrated only in Christianity. For where else is death accomplished with consent as the gate of life, and does not become mere chance or an abyss of secret despair? And, on the other hand, the doctrine and the achievement of a just death cannot be considered a mere incidental in the religion of one who died on the cross. This hidden correspondence is not found anywhere else. It is no wonder that, on the whole, we find only in Christianity this voluntary death on an historically sufficient scale, on the public stage of history as it were.

We can, therefore, say that if such a death by its own characteristics shows itself to be a good one, a death of matured, achieved freedom and not a death of frustrated freedom, of an ontologically and personally crippled freedom; and, furthermore, if this death is, in fact, undergone in the presence of Christianity, for the sake of it, and in directly perceptible correspondence with its doctrines; and if this death nowhere else occurs, at least to this extent, a fact which must have

113

a reason; then all this can be explained only because this good death of accomplished freedom draws its strength from the motive for which the man dies. In other words: this death is good, because it occurs for the sake of Christ who was crucified and died.

The good death thus becomes the witness to a good cause. It is really a testimony to the truth. There can be a death in which the subjective character of the dying testifies (before God and in the depths of man) that the death is better than the concrete thing for which death is accepted; that there is discord between the objective side (the objectively proposed motive) and the subjective side (what is personally achieved in death). However, for the reasons mentioned previously, this does not apply in the case of martyrdom, as actually observed in the history of Christianity.

We have merely been able to suggest various points. Several statements have been made which require more detailed demonstration. Because our thoughts are far away from death, and not under the immediate impression of the testimony given by a freely accepted death, many things which a death itself can say very simply and in silence, needed rather discursive explanation. It must also be remembered that all the testimonies which awaken faith and all the motives of credibility are motives of *credibility*, not demonstrative arguments which, by-passing man's free decision, conclude automatically and aim at compelling his assent, as would be the case with mathematical or physical demonstrations. At all events what has been said may have made it clear why death is particularly apt to become the event in which objective and subjective goodness can no longer be in disharmony, and why death, in its natural, personal essence, has a *potentia obedientialis* to function as a testimony to the faith, being, as it is, the summit of the act of faith, which can be adequately interpreted only through this faith.

Arriving at the conclusion of our argument, its basic outline could be summarized formally as follows. In the abstract, the essences of those realities and achievements (especially and primarily those of men) of which we can have empirical knowledge are found in different cases and in different realizations. As physical or personal "natural" realities, they are not by themselves witnesses to the fact that God's hand is here at work. However, in the concrete, they can occur in such a configuration and in such a way as to require a sufficient reason and meaning which cannot be found on the natural level. If, for example, we observe that a particular configuration in fact only occurs in conjunction with something else, then it bears witness to that other thing. If therefore the essence of death appears in its purity only in Christian death, then, through this connection, the Christian element for which and on the basis of which man dies, is testified to as well. Of course, from this brief outline one basic difficulty is apparent (of a concrete and particular, not of a theoretical kind), namely: death as the pure, radiant, adequately authenticated accomplishment of human reality is recognized as such in fact only by one who is in his heart already (perhaps without even knowing it) in accord with what he sees, that is, who is himself already a Christian. For how could anybody, for instance, recognize the death of the martyr as a death demonstrating its purity and goodness, other than by living with fundamentally the same attitude, by undergoing the same death spiritually in himself, and by being ready to accept the same death freely and in the confidence of faith? Nevertheless, such an event is a motive of faith because in principle it can be known "naturally", since it is a natural and empirical reality. Thus every man, in so far as he has not finally closed himself to the possibility of development (which can be done only by an evil death), still has in himself enough capacity for understanding as to be able, once his attention is aroused by the event in question, to grow into comprehension. Consequently it is not a false paradox to say (considering man dynamically and not freezing him into a static concept) that only the believer has understood the motive of faith and yet the motive of faith is the ground of faith. Faith and the understanding of its motive grow together. The basic condition, which as a real possibility already exists, although not yet actually accepted, lies in the essence of man, which even the wickedest decision can never totally enslave, and in the grace of God, which makes a man see at least something even when he really does not wish to see, and remains in a position to suppress or repress the emerging insight.

After this short digression, we proceed with our reflections on martyrdom. It is, we have said, the highest personal event in the Christian life because, deriving from faith and furnishing a testimony to faith, in it the highest deed of man and its historical manifestation before the eyes of the Church and of the world coalesce into one, in an absolute (one might almost say "supra-sacramental") manner.

It is no wonder that throughout the history of the Church there have always been Christians longing for martyrdom and praying to God for this greatest of all graces. It is no wonder ment which murder the person before the body, and take a man completely from himself, is an even more intense participation in the death of Christ than another martyrdom more heroic in appearance? When we depict the martyr on the model of Christ, the martyr of our own times resembles the Lord no more and no less than those of the past: the martyr who is lying on the ground suffocated by his own mortal weakness; the martyr who feels he is forsaken by God; or the martyr hanging almost indistinguishably among real criminals; the martyr who is almost convinced that he is not a martyr at all; the martyr who cannot and yet does fulfil what he does not find the strength in himself to fulfil; the martyr who is perhaps *ad metalla damnatus* (condemned to the mines) for life and thus condemned may die an apparently normal death. And today the *metalla* need not be any particular place, for the gaol may coincide with the land of godless tyranny as such.

One might almost think that Christian life can be understood only in the light of Christian death in its absolute sense, that is, in martyrdom, and that the poverty and aridity of our modern Christian existence is revealed in the discouraging fact that there is so little courage in us for such a vocation. Therefore, it is good for us to look to Jesus, to the source and the consummation of our faith, who, in spite of the joy that was his, and in spite of the ignominy, endured the cross (Heb 12:2), and to strengthen our hearts by praying for this grace of a faithful heart, while looking to all those who in all truth manifestly preceded us in the sign of faith, those who bore witness in the past and in recent days of the Church. Today, as we speak, millions are suffering for the name of Jesus. They suffer, believing and enduring, unknown and without fame, atoning also for our guilt of cowardly indifference, weakness of faith, pleasure-seeking mediocrity. They are the victims on whom we live; they go the way which may suddenly become for us too the only road that leads to life; they experience the vocation which in deepest reality is also ours, because we also have been baptized into the death of the Lord, and we also receive in the sacrament of the altar the body which was given up to death for us. They are the true followers of the Lord in whom he himself suffers and dies, the images of true love, as Polycarp called them. We wish we could say today what the great Origen once said in his community: "I have no doubt that in this community there are a number of Christians – God alone knows them – who before him, according to the testimony of their consciences, are already martyrs, who are ready, as soon as it is asked of them, to shed their blood for Christ. I have no doubt that there are amongst us many who have already taken their cross upon themselves and have followed him" (*Hom. in Num.* 10:2). "Δὸς αἶμα καὶ λαβὲ πνεῦμα" (Give the blood and take the spirit) is an old monastic saying. This is also true today. As the Spirit and the water of eternal life flowed from the pierced heart of the Lord, so, too, the Spirit in the Church will always depend upon there being those in the Church who are prepared for martyrdom. And just as, amidst the weakness and misery of men, the Spirit, through his own victorious strength, provides that man's cowardly laziness should not extinguish the Spirit in the Church, he also provides that in the Church, again and again death is that terrible and blessed event, in which glorious testimony is borne that man freely believes and by such an act of total freedom in faith, enters by grace into the infinite freedom of God.